Pakistan

Pakistan

By Liz Sonneborn

Enchantment of the World™
Second Series

Children's Press®

An Imprint of Scholastic Inc.

NEW YORK   TORONTO   LONDON   AUCKLAND   SYDNEY
MEXICO CITY   NEW DELHI   HONG KONG
DANBURY, CONNECTICUT

Frontispiece: Badshahi Mosque, Lahore

Consultant: Tahir Naqvi, Assistant Professor, Department of Sociology and Anthropology, Trinity University, San Antonio, Texas

Please note: All statistics are as up-to-date as possible at the time of publication.

Book production by The Design Lab

Library of Congress Cataloging-in-Publication Data
Sonneborn, Liz.
  Pakistan/by Liz Sonneborn.
      p. cm.—(Enchantment of the world, second series)
  Includes bibliographical references and index.
  ISBN: 978-0-531-27544-3 (lib. bdg.)
  1. Pakistan—Juvenile literature. I. Title.
  DS376.9.S66 2013
  954.91—dc23   2012000505

1 2 3 4 5 6 7 8 9 10 R 22 21 20 19 18 17 16 15 14 13

Pakistan

Contents

Cover photo:
Woman with child
and water container

Indus River

Markhors

Ancient City, Modern Nation

IN 1922, RAKHAL DAS BANERJI TRAVELED TO A REMOTE area along the Indus River in what was then India and is now part of Pakistan. Banerji was an archaeologist, a scientist who studies ancient artifacts and buildings to learn about how people once lived. He was working for the government of Great Britain, which controlled India at that time.

Banerji was curious about a place known as Mohenjo Daro, which means "mound of the dead" in the Sindhi language. He had heard that it housed the ruins of a Buddhist stupa, or shrine. At the site of the ruins, he found a tool made out of a dark mineral called flint. Banerji had a hunch that the tool was far older than the shrine. He asked his superiors for permission to dig in the area to search for other objects.

Discovering a Civilization

What Banerji discovered was amazing. Buried under the stupa and the nearby overgrown hillsides was a forgotten city. Through a series of digs over many decades, archaeologists

Opposite: **The city of Mohenjo Daro reached its peak about four thousand years ago. Excavation of its ruins did not begin until the 1930s.**

Many different animals were depicted on seals from Mohenjo Daro, including rhinoceroses, tigers, and bulls.

found that the city at Mohenjo Daro stretched over some 250 acres (100 hectares).

While digging in the area, Banerji uncovered several stone and metal seals, or stamps, carved with pictures of animals and a form of writing. Similar seals had been found at Harappa, a village about 400 miles (650 kilometers) to the north. The seals, therefore, indicated that Mohenjo Daro was just one of several cities that had once been occupied by people with a shared culture.

When pictures of Banerji's seals were published, British archaeologists immediately noticed something interesting.

They looked just like seals discovered in the ruins of ancient Sumer, which had flourished more than three thousand years before in what is now Iraq. The archaeologists decided that the people of Sumer must have traded goods with people from the Mohenjo Daro area.

This discovery caused the archaeologists to realize the importance of the ruins of Mohenjo Daro. The ruins were evidence that the Indus River valley had been home to a great civilization thousands of years before. This civilization, now often called the Harappan culture, had been forgotten over the centuries. Archaeologists eventually determined that Mohenjo Daro, though inhabited for about one thousand years, was at its height between 2600 and 1900 BCE. It was likely the first city in all of South Asia.

The Harappan Culture

Archaeologists have continued to study the ruins of Mohenjo Daro to find out more about the city and the people who lived there. Unlike most ancient cities, Mohenjo Daro was not a disorganized collection of streets and buildings, constructed at random as the city grew. Instead, the city's streets were arranged in a neat grid, with large parallel thoroughfares connected by smaller streets at right angles. The streets and the houses were built from baked mud bricks. Remarkably, the bricks were identical in size and shape. These standardized bricks suggest that the construction of Mohenjo Daro was carefully planned and carried out by officials and laborers working for some kind of central government.

The city had a massive drainage system, which is more evidence of its orderly society. The elaborate system made the most of the area's small water supply. It sent water into every home in the city, each of which had its own bathing area.

The Great Bath was the largest building in the city. Its giant pool may have been used for religious rituals. The people who built the bath carefully sealed the pool's bricks together with asphalt to keep it from leaking.

This ceramic oxcart was found in Mohenjo Daro. Experts are not sure what purpose this sculpture served. It may have been a toy.

At Mohenjo Daro, archaeologists have found many everyday objects that shed light on daily life there. These items include jewelry, pottery, tools made of copper and stone, weights used to measure trade goods, and children's toys crafted out of clay. These artifacts make clear that the people of Mohenjo Daro included farmers, craftspeople, and merchants.

Probably the most famous artifact excavated at Mohenjo Daro is a small bronze figurine known as Dancing Girl. It depicts a confident teenage girl, with her hand on her hip and her head held high.

Another important find is an intricately carved sculpture of a man. It is sometimes called Priest-King, because the man's dignified look suggests that he is an important person.

Despite the name given to this statue, there is no evidence that Mohenjo Daro was ruled by kings or religious leaders. If it had been, the remains of palaces or temples would likely have been found among the ruins. Instead, most archaeologists think that power over Mohenjo Daro was shared by a group of elites or maybe even elected officials.

Dancing Girl is only about 4 inches (10 centimeters) tall.

Old and New

Today, the site of Mohenjo Daro is located in southern Pakistan, a country that was created in 1947. Although thousands of years have passed since the ancient city's decline, in some small ways, life there has not changed too dramatically. Many Pakistanis living near the ruins still farm the fertile lands of the Indus River valley, just like the residents of Mohenjo Daro did. In fact, contemporary farmers there often plant the same crops and raise the same animals that their counterparts did in ancient times.

Mohenjo Daro may be in ruins, but Pakistan is now home to some of the biggest cities in South Asia. They feature tall buildings, highways, and modern conveniences that no resident of Mohenjo Daro could have imagined. The size of Pakistan's largest city, Karachi, certainly dwarfs that of Mohenjo Daro. At its height, Mohenjo Daro may have housed as many as forty thousand people, while Karachi is home to thirteen million people.

Although it's impossible to know everything about the people of Mohenjo Daro, what they left behind suggests they lived in a stable and orderly society. Unfortunately, in modern times, Pakistanis have often not been so lucky. During its short history, Pakistan has suffered many struggles—from civil war to ethnic strife to severe poverty to rule by brutal military dictators. The Pakistani people of today face a difficult challenge as they try to leave behind their troubled past and move toward a more promising future.

The Merewether Clock Tower is an important landmark in Karachi, Pakistan's largest city.

High and Dry

PAKISTAN IS LOCATED IN SOUTHERN ASIA ON THE Indian subcontinent—an enormous peninsula south of the Himalaya Mountains that juts into the Indian Ocean. Pakistan shares the subcontinent with two other nations: India and Bangladesh.

Four countries border Pakistan: Iran lies to the west; Afghanistan to the north and west; China to the north; and India to the east. Pakistan's southern border rests on the Arabian Sea, a part of the Indian Ocean.

According to the borders recognized by the United Nations, an international peacekeeping organization, Pakistan stretches over an area of 307,374 square miles (796,095 sq km). But Pakistan's government claims land in the area traditionally called Kashmir. This area includes Jammu and Kashmir, a state that is officially part of India. The portions of Kashmir that are now controlled by Pakistan are called Azad (meaning "free") Kashmir and Gilgit-Baltistan. They measure 4,494 square miles (11,639 sq km) and 28,000 square miles (72,520 sq km), respectively.

Opposite: **The rocky Himalayas tower over the valleys in Azad Kashmir.**

Pakistan's Geographic Features

Highest Elevation: K2, 28,251 feet (8,611 m) above sea level

Lowest Elevation: Indian Ocean, sea level

Longest River: Indus River, 1,708 miles (2,749 km) within Pakistan

Largest Lake: Manchhar Lake, 200 square miles (520 sq km) when full

Longest Border: With India, 1,809 miles (2,911 km)

Shortest Border: With China, 325 miles (523 km)

Length of Coastline: 650 miles (1,046 km)

Hottest Month: June, average high temperature of 106°F (41°C)

Coldest Month: January, average low temperature of 41°F (5°C)

Wettest Month: July, average annual rainfall in Karachi of 3.8 inches (9.7 cm)

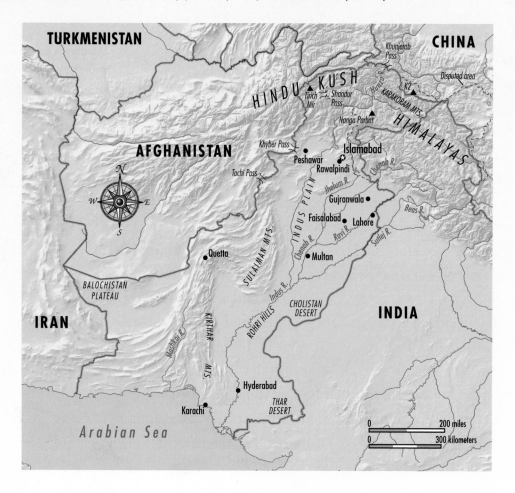

The Indus River Plains

Pakistan features a wide variety of landscapes, from arid deserts to snowy mountaintops. The highest elevations in Pakistan are found in the north and northwest in the Himalayan and Karakoram mountain ranges. K2, the second-highest mountain in the world after Mount Everest, is found in Gilgit-Baltistan. In addition to mountains, the northern highlands also feature lush pine forests and green valleys.

To the south are the fertile Indus River plains. The Indus River is 1,980 miles (3,185 km) long. Originating in China, it runs through central Pakistan before emptying into the Arabian Sea. Many rivers feed into the Indus. These include

The Indus River winds along the entire length of Pakistan.

Camels are well adapted to the hot, dry Cholistan Desert. Hundreds of thousands of camels live there.

the Kabul River to the west and the Jhelum, Chenab, Ravi, and Sutlej Rivers to the east.

The plain on the eastern side of the Indus is the most fertile area in Pakistan. Most of the nation's farmland is in this region. Much of this land is irrigated with water from the Indus and its tributaries. It is also the most populated area of Pakistan. About 70 percent of all Pakistanis live in the Indus Plain.

In central and southeastern Pakistan, the plains border desert lands. The Thar and Cholistan Deserts are forbidding environments. The Cholistan lies north of the larger Thar Desert, which extends into western India. Sand dunes and ridges carpet these deserts.

Cities in Pakistan

A little more than one-third of Pakistanis live in urban areas. The largest city in the country is Karachi (below). In fact, with more than 13 million people, it is one of the most populous cities in the world. It grew quickly after Pakistan and India became independent from Great Britain in 1947. Pakistan was created as a predominantly Muslim nation, and many Muslims from India moved to Karachi. Karachi is the capital of the Sindh province. It is located in southern Pakistan along the coast of the Arabian Sea. As Pakistan's primary port, nearly all goods being shipped in or out of the country pass through the city. Karachi is also the center of industry, banking, and communications in Pakistan.

Far to the northeast is Pakistan's second-largest city, Lahore. It is located on fertile lands along the Ravi River, just a few miles from Pakistan's border with India. With a population of more than 7 million, Lahore

has a healthy economy focused on agriculture and manufacturing. It also serves as an important cultural and educational center. In addition to its museums and libraries, Lahore is home to University of the Punjab, one of Pakistan's oldest universities. The city's landmarks include several excellent examples of Mughal architecture dating from the seventeenth century. Among them are the great pavilion called the Shish Mahal and the Badshahi Mosque (above), which is one of the largest Islamic houses of worship in the world.

About 62 miles (100 km) to the west of Lahore is Faisalabad, Pakistan's third-largest city, with about 3 million people. Farmland surrounding the city produces cotton, wheat, vegetables, and sugarcane. Textile manufacturing is also a leading industry in the area.

At the base of the Himalayas lies Pakistan's fourth-biggest city, Rawalpindi, home to about 1.5 million people. The city's industrial plants produce oil, iron, chemicals, and furniture, among other goods. The city is also the headquarters of Pakistan's army. Rawalpindi served as the nation's capital from 1959 to 1967. The new capital, Islamabad, is just 9 miles (15 km) from Rawalpindi, which allows the two cities to have close ties economically and culturally.

To the west of the Indus are the Sulaiman and Kirthar mountain ranges. Beyond these mountains is a large flat area called the Balochistan Plateau. This plateau region has an average elevation of more than 1,000 feet (300 meters). The area is so dry that few people live there. At the foot of some hills, however, there is enough water to support small villages of farmers and shepherds.

Climate

Like the landscape, the climate of Pakistan varies from place to place. In the high mountains of the north, for instance, conditions are similar to those of Arctic regions. In the extreme southeast, the climate is unbearably hot and dry.

The northwest, where many people live, is the most temperate part of Pakistan, although winter temperatures often

The Karakoram Highway

Pakistan is home to one of the twentieth century's greatest engineering achievements—the Karakoram Highway (KKH). This road, which links northern Pakistan and western China, follows a route pioneered by ancient traders. Constructed in the 1960s and 1970s with the help of the Chinese government, the highway was built by blasting through the enormous hills and mountains of the region. The KKH runs for about 800 miles (1,300 km), weaving through great ravines, high mountains, and treacherous passes. Because of its incredible views, the KKH attracts many backpackers, bicyclists, and other adventurous tourists.

Abbottabad

Nestled in the Sarban Hills of northeastern Pakistan is the town of Abbottabad. It was founded by James Abbott in January 1853, when the British controlled the region. Abbott was a major in the British army, and he established the town as a military camp. Four months later, Abbott was sent to another post. Before leaving, he wrote a poem about the town that bears his name. It included the lines:

Oh, Abbottabad, we are leaving you now
To your natural beauty do I bow
Perhaps your wind's sound will never reach my ear
My gift for you is a few sad tears
I bid you farewell with a heavy heart
Never from my mind will your memories thwart

Today, the poem appears on a plaque in a park in Abbottabad.

Abbottabad has long been known for its beautiful views and pleasant weather. Then, in early May 2011, it made headlines for a different reason. Osama bin Laden, the mastermind behind the terrorist attacks on the United States on September 11, 2001, was killed by American soldiers at his hideout in Abbottabad.

drop below freezing. Central Pakistan is generally much hotter, with the thermometer sometimes topping 122 degrees Fahrenheit (50 degrees Celsius) in the warmest months. The coast of Pakistan is also warm, although sea breezes can make it feel cooler.

Pakistan has roughly three seasons. October to February is the coolest and driest time of year. March to June is generally hot and humid. During this time, the plains often experience violent dust storms called the Kali Andhi. These storms are so severe that they block out the sun and make it difficult

Dust storms make it difficult to breathe and see. They can ground airplane flights and stop traffic.

to see anything. July to September is the monsoon season. Monsoons are winds from the ocean that carry heavy rains and are followed by extreme humidity. When the sun comes out after a monsoon, the air feels hot and sticky.

Monsoon rains can be a welcome relief from the hot summer temperatures. But sometimes they lead to disaster. In 2010, for instance, the rains were so heavy that the Indus overflowed its banks. Pakistan suffered its worst flooding in decades. Almost two thousand people died, and many buildings and roads were destroyed. In all, the catastrophic flooding affected the lives of some twenty million Pakistanis.

Pakistanis forced from their homes wade through floodwaters in 2010. It was the nation's worst flooding since 1929.

Into the Wild

FROM DESERTS TO RIVER VALLEYS TO TOWERING mountains, Pakistan is a land of many different environments. Given its diverse habitats, the country is home to a wide variety of plants and animals.

Opposite: **Autumn leaves brighten the land in Khaplu, in northeastern Pakistan.**

Plant Life

The most appealing environment for plants is found in the mountainous north. Unlike most of Pakistan, this region receives enough rainfall to allow trees and small plants to flourish. Pakistan's greatest natural forests are found in the southern ranges of the Himalayas. There, below the snow line, hillsides are covered with pines, poplars, and willows. The area also features dense forests of deodar cedars. Also known as the Himalayan cedar, the deodar cedar is the national tree of Pakistan. This large evergreen often grows as high as 150 feet (50 m) and has a trunk that measures about 10 feet (3 m) in diameter. In the city of Abbottabad, some of the largest deodar cedars are more than two hundred years old.

Jasmine

Pakistan's national plant is the common jasmine, whose beautiful white blossoms have long been associated with Pakistan and India. It is often called poet's jasmine, because of its frequent appearance in the traditional poetry of the region. Famous for their sweet smell, jasmine flowers are often used to make perfume and natural medicines. The official state seal of Pakistan features a wreath of jasmine surrounding a coat of arms that displays images of the country's leading crop plants.

Although drier than the mountainous region, the Balochistan Plateau supports the second-largest juniper forest in the world. The forest is believed to be nearly five thousand years old. Each year, the trees' berries produce thousands of tons of oil, which is used to make perfume. The plateau also sustains coarse grasses, dwarf palms, and other smaller plants that can survive in its arid climate.

Few wild plants grow in the hot Indus River plains. The area is hospitable to only the hardiest grasses, bushes, and thorn trees. But in many places, this natural vegetation has been stripped away to create irrigated fields. There, farmers grow wheat in the winter and cotton and rice in the summer.

Through irrigation, the government of Pakistan also maintains several forests on lands that otherwise could not sustain trees. The Changa Manga, for instance, is one of the largest irrigated forests in the world. Planted mostly with kikar and mulberry trees, it covers approximately 12,510 acres (5,000 ha) south of Lahore. It was first planted by the British to provide lumber as fuel for the region's railway system. Today, it is a popular park area where families gather to picnic and ride a miniature train through the forest.

Animal Life

Northern Pakistan is home to some of Asia's most exotic animals. The Marco Polo sheep, for instance, is known for its distinctive, curving horns, which can grow up to 6 feet (1.8 m) long. These sheep can survive on very high mountains despite the extreme cold winds that howl across the land. Other wild sheep and goats native to Pakistan include the urial sheep, the Siberian ibex, and the markhor, which is Pakistan's national animal.

Marco Polo sheep live high in the mountains, at elevations above 12,000 feet (3,700 m).

The Markhor

The mountainous regions of northern Pakistan are home to the markhor, the country's national animal. Markhors spend some twelve hours a day grazing on grasses, leaves, or twigs. Although they live on a vegetarian diet, their name comes from the Persian words for "snake eating."

A member of the goat family, the hefty markhor can weigh up to 240 pounds (110 kilograms). Aside from its size, the markhor's most distinguishing characteristics are the long woolly mane found on males and the tall spiral horns found on both sexes. These horns sometimes reach 5 feet (1.5 m) long.

Hunters have long preyed on markhors in the hope of making a trophy of the horns. In China and other nations, markhor horns are also used to make medicines. In part because of overhunting, the markhor is an endangered species. Only a few thousand markhors now live in the wild.

Several rare types of mammals also live in the mountainous north. These include the snow leopard, which has long, thick fur that keeps it warm in the frigid environment. Snow leopards usually hunt at night and are rarely seen in the wild. They are surprisingly agile for their size. A snow leopard can easily leap 12 feet (4 m) into the air.

The Himalayan black bear also lives in the northern forests. These bears can be identified by the V-shaped patches of white fur on their chests. Although these bears eat insects for the most part, they have been known to kill and eat large animals, such as goats and wild boar.

Large mammals common in the Indus River plains include jackals, hyenas, and foxes. Deer, boar, and otters are found in the southern wetlands. Even the harsh Cholistan Desert is home to many large mammals, including gazelles, foxes, wolves, and mongooses. In farming areas, buffalo are often raised for their milk, while cattle and sometimes camels are used to pull plows. Throughout rural Pakistan, carts drawn by donkeys are a common form of transportation.

Birds, Reptiles, and Fish

Many types of birds live in Pakistan. Crows, sparrows, hawks, falcons, and eagles are all common. The lakes and wetlands in

A donkey pulls a cart loaded with plastic jugs. There are more than four million donkeys in Pakistan.

Adult flamingos turn pink or red, depending on their diet. The more carotenoid nutrients they eat, the more brightly colored they become.

the southern portion of the country are a paradise for waterfowl, such as ducks and geese. Pelicans, flamingos, and ibises live along the shore of the Arabian Sea.

The Indus River Dolphin

A rare species of dolphin lives in the waters of the Indus River in central Pakistan. Measuring up to 8 feet (2.5 m) in length, the Indus River dolphin has a long, narrow beak and wide flippers. It is nearly blind—its eyes have no lenses and only a tiny opening to allow in light. Eyesight is fairly useless to the dolphin in the murky waters of the Indus. The dolphin instead navigates the river by relying on echolocation, the same system bats use. The dolphin sends out calls and then listens to the echoes reflected when the sound waves hit objects. Using echolocation, the dolphin can avoid hitting boats and find fish to eat. The Indus River dolphin is now endangered. Only about 1,100 of them survive in Pakistan. Conservationists are working to help stop the number of these dolphins from dwindling.

The wetlands are home to many species of reptiles and fish as well. Crocodiles crawl through the marshes near Karachi, Pakistan's largest city. The Indus and other rivers are full of freshwater fish, such as the ilish (also known as the palla fish) and the snow trout. In coastal waters, fishers catch mackerels, herrings, and sharks. Along the shore, they also collect crabs, shrimps, and many other types of edible shellfish.

Protecting Wildlife

In recent years, the Pakistani population has grown rapidly. As cities and villages have expanded, they have destroyed the

The Sheedi people of Pakistan believe crocodiles are sacred. During an annual festival near Karachi, they feed the giant creatures.

Car exhaust is one of the major causes of air pollution in Pakistan.

habitats of many animals. Pakistani wildlife also faces other serious threats. Some large mammals are in danger of extinction in part because they have been overhunted. At the same time, forest animals are struggling to survive, as many Pakistanis legally or illegally cut down trees to use as fuel or lumber. Much of Pakistan is also growing more and more polluted. Car exhaust, especially near cities, makes the air unhealthy to breathe. Also, Pakistan's rivers and lakes are polluted with sewage and industrial waste.

Many of Pakistan's environmental problems can be traced to its unstable government, which has been unable and sometimes unwilling to protect threatened habitats. As a result, some of the animals most associated with Pakistan are endangered, including the snow leopard, the Marco Polo sheep, and the Himalayan black bear. Some types of plants have also been damaged by human activity and the growth of cities. The juniper forests of the Balochistan Plateau, for example, are growing smaller each year because the trees are harvested illegally.

Pakistan's government has tried to preserve some endangered areas and species through its parks program. Pakistan now has twenty-five national parks and about two hundred wildlife sanctuaries and game reserves. Hunting, clearing land, and polluting the water are all prohibited in the parks in an effort to protect the natural animal and plant life. Millions of Pakistanis and foreign tourists visit these parks each year to experience Pakistan's rich and varied natural heritage.

Saving Turtles

Sandspit Beach on the Arabian Sea is a traditional nesting ground for the green turtle and the olive ridley turtle, two of the eight species of sea turtles. Unfortunately, these large reptiles are in danger of extinction, in part because Sandspit is overrun by beachgoers from nearby Karachi. The World Wildlife Fund is now working with Karachi's government to operate the Save the Turtle Project. The program calls on students, teachers, and other volunteers to help clean up litter left on the turtles' nesting grounds. The group is particularly concerned about stray plastic bags. Turtles often chomp on the bags, which they mistake for jellyfish, one of their favorite foods. The bags can cause deadly blockages inside their bodies.

Past and Present

THE FIRST CIVILIZATION IN WHAT IS NOW PAKISTAN emerged in about 3000 BCE. The Harappan culture was centered on the fertile lands near the Indus River. While most Harappans lived in small villages, many people dwelled in large cities at the civilization's height. Harappa and Mohenjo Daro each had about forty thousand residents. The Harappans supported their large population by irrigating farmland.

By about 1500 BCE, the Harappan culture had declined, and its great cities were abandoned. Its collapse was probably due to a changing climate that caused much of the Indus River valley to dry up.

Foreign Influences

After the Indus valley civilization came to an end, the region fell prey to a series of foreign invaders. These included Aryans from the north, who began moving into the area around 1700 BCE. They brought with them the Sanskrit language, an ancestor of the languages many Pakistanis now speak. The Aryan

Opposite: **A figure called Priest-King was discovered at Mohenjo Daro. The stone sculpture is about 6.9 inches (17.5 cm) tall.**

The Buddhist religion spread across the Indian subcontinent during the Mauryan Empire. Many religious monuments, like this one in what is now Sanchi, India, were built in the region.

invaders also introduced religious beliefs that eventually developed into Hinduism, now the dominant religion of India.

Around 300 BCE, what is now Pakistan became part of the Mauryan Empire, which was based in northern India. The Mauryan rulers eventually controlled the entire Indian subcontinent. After the breakup of the Mauryan Empire in the second century BCE, the region came under the control of various other peoples, including the Kushans, the Sassanians, and the Huns.

In 711 CE, an Arab general named Muhammad bin Qasim led thousands of soldiers into what is now the Sindh province of southern Pakistan. The event marked an important moment in the history of Pakistan, because this was when the

Arabs introduced Islam to the region. The religion of Islam remains an important force in Pakistan's politics, culture, and society. Today, nearly all Pakistanis are Muslims, people who practice Islam.

The Mughals and the British

Starting in the sixteenth century, the entire subcontinent once again became part of a vast empire. The Mughals moved into the region from central Asia and gained control of what is now Pakistan. They ruled for some three hundred years. Under

Empires and Invasions

☐ Mauryan Empire, 260 BCE	☐ Sassanian Empire, 642 CE
☐ Kushan Empire, 200 CE	☐ Mughal Empire, 1707 CE
→ Arab invasions, 711 CE	→ Aryan invasions, 1500 BCE
☐ Present-day Pakistan	

Babur (standing at right in gold) founded the Mughal Empire. He had gardens built throughout the empire.

Lahore Fort

One of the greatest architectural wonders of Pakistan is the Lahore Fort. The fort was constructed during the Mughal civilization, which reached its height in the sixteenth and seventeenth centuries. Within the fort's walls are several monuments, palaces, and mosques. Many are made of the finest marble and decorated with semiprecious stones and mosaics (images and decorations made from bits of glass or stone). Among the fort's most impressive structures is the Shish Mahal. Constructed during the reign of Mughal ruler Shah Jahan, its name means "crystal palace" in the Urdu language. Because the Shish Mahal's white marble walls and ceilings are inlaid with small mirrors, it is known as the Palace of Mirrors. Shalamar Gardens was also built by Shah Jahan. Stretching over 40 acres (16 ha), the gardens are arranged over three levels and feature ponds and waterfalls.

the great emperor Akbar, Lahore was the Mughal capital. There, Mughal rulers built some of the most magnificent buildings in the country, including the Badshahi Mosque and Jahangir's Tomb.

By the early 1700s, the Mughal emperors began to lose their influence. As Mughal control declined, a new group of foreigners—the British—became the dominant force in the subcontinent. The first British in the region were traders. As long as they were making money, they were happy to make deals with the Mughal emperor and local leaders, and they stayed out the region's politics. The attitude of the British changed, however, after the Indian Rebellion of 1857. During the rebellion, the people in what is now central India rose up against the British. After the British put down the revolt, the

British government removed the last Mughal emperor from power and took political control of the emperor's lands.

In British-controlled India (which included present-day Pakistan), English became the official language. Many Muslims who spoke other languages, such as Urdu and Persian, were shut out of positions in the government. Muslims had lost a great deal of political power after the British takeover, so Muslims were seen as being particularly hostile to the British. Because of this, the British also favored subjects who practiced the Hindu religion and gave them greater access to power. As a result, many Muslims in India came to resent the Hindus as much as they resented the British.

During the Indian Rebellion, British soldiers stormed Delhi, where many of the rebels had gathered.

Poet and Visionary

Muhammad Iqbal, the visionary who first imagined the Muslim state of Pakistan, was born in 1877, in the town of Sialkot, in what is now northeastern Pakistan. After attending college in Lahore, he began teaching and writing poetry. He soon traveled to England and Germany to earn a doctorate. In Europe, he became intrigued by the writings of Western philosophers. Iqbal became well known for his poetry, written in Urdu and Persian, and for his philosophical essays. He was knighted by the king of England in 1922.

Returning to India, Iqbal became increasingly involved in politics. He was elected to the legislature of the Indian province of Punjab. Iqbal also became active in the All-India Muslim League, an organization of Indian Muslims founded in 1906 that sought to

free India from British rule. In 1930, Iqbal delivered a historic speech at the league's annual conference. Imagining an independent India, he called for the formation of a Muslim state, in which the rights of India's Muslim minority would be protected from the country's Hindu majority. Iqbal's notion of a Muslim state carved out of India eventually gave birth to an even bigger idea—an entirely new Muslim country that would become known as Pakistan.

Iqbal died in 1938, nine years before his dream was realized. He was buried near the Badshahi Mosque in Lahore. Because of Iqbal's role in creating the country, Pakistanis celebrate his birthday as a national holiday.

Many Indians, both Muslim and Hindu, were unhappy with British rule. They wanted more control over their government. Eventually, they began fighting to make India an independent nation. Initially, Muslim and Hindu leaders worked together toward this goal.

In 1930, however, Muhammad Iqbal, a Muslim poet and philosopher from Lahore, gave a speech proposing that an independent India include a separate state reserved for Muslims. He believed the Muslim minority needed protection from political, economic, and social discrimination by the Hindu majority. Mohammed Ali Jinnah, the leader of the All-India Muslim League political party, embraced and expanded Iqbal's idea. Jinnah wanted British-controlled India to become two separate countries—Hindu-dominated India and Muslim-dominated Pakistan. At its annual meeting in 1940, the Muslim League formally supported this plan. It was still not clear, however, whether Pakistan would be an independent nation or a group of Muslim states within India.

Mohammed Ali Jinnah promoted the idea of dividing India into two separate nations.

A New Nation

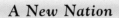

By the end of World War II (1939–1945), Great Britain could no longer afford to rule India. In July 1947, it agreed to transfer power to the Indian people. Britain also agreed to the demand of Muslims that they be granted their own

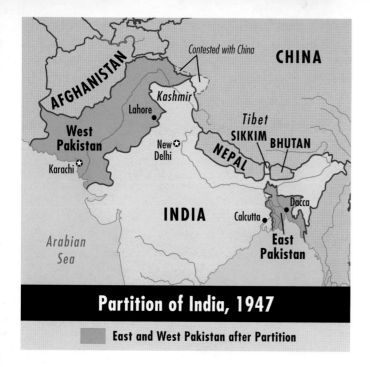

Partition of India, 1947

East and West Pakistan after Partition

homeland. This division of India into two nations is known as Partition.

On August 14, 1947, Pakistan became an independent nation. Jinnah was appointed governor-general, which was largely a ceremonial post. Liaquat Ali Khan, another important leader in the Muslim League, became the country's first prime minister.

British officials had hastily drawn up the borders between Pakistan and India. Pakistan was made up of two parts—East Pakistan and West Pakistan. Both regions were dominated by Muslims, but they did not share any borders. Instead, they were separated by more than 1,000 miles (1,600 km) of land that was now part of independent India. Although most of the people in these two areas shared a religion, they belonged to different ethnic

Naming Pakistan

The name Pakistan was suggested in 1933 by Chaudhry Rahmat Ali, a young Indian man studying at the University of Cambridge in England. In a pamphlet titled *Now or Never*, he made a case for creating a Muslim-dominated state from land in British-held India. Ali urged the British and Indian officials who were working toward Indian independence to remember the needs of those in "PAKSTAN." He created this name by taking letters from the five regions of northern India that were dominated by Muslims: Punjab, Afghan province (now Khyber Pakhtunkhwa province), Kashmir, Sindh, and Balochistan. An "I" was later inserted into Ali's suggested name so that it was easier to pronounce. In addition to being an acronym made up from letters of the Muslim regions, *Pakistan* also means "land of the pure" in the Persian and Urdu languages.

groups. The people of East Pakistan were Bengalis, while the people of West Pakistan were mostly Punjabis and Sindhis. Given their geographical distance and ethnic differences, it was hard for the people of East and West Pakistan to see themselves as belonging to a unified nation.

When the partitioning of British-controlled India was announced, it set off one of the biggest migrations in modern history. Hindus living in Pakistan wanted to move to India, while Muslims living in India wanted to move to Pakistan. The migrants said good-bye to their jobs, homes, and

People crowd into and on top of a train that is heading to Pakistan from New Delhi, India, shortly after India was partitioned. Millions of people moved between India and Pakistan during that period.

communities and then headed off by train or by foot. By some estimates, twenty-five million people crossed the new border between India and Pakistan. It was a chaotic situation, and violence often broke out between the groups. In the years following the separation of Pakistan and India, as many as one million people were killed.

Another problem created by Partition was the battle for Kashmir. Even though the population in Kashmir was primarily Muslim, it was assigned to India rather than Pakistan. Pakistan refused to give up its claims to Kashmir. In 1947, 1965, and 1999, Pakistan and India went to war over the region, but the boundary dispute has yet to be fully resolved.

Pakistanis protest in the streets, demanding that India give up Kashmir. Pakistan and India have battled over Kashmir since their borders were defined in 1947.

Prime Minister Liaquat Ali Khan was assassinated by an Afghan extremist at a Muslim League meeting in 1951.

Struggles and Challenges

In its early years, Pakistan was troubled by a lack of leadership. Jinnah, considered the founder of Pakistan, died in 1948, just thirteen months after the country became independent. Prime Minister Liaquat Ali Khan was assassinated three years later. After the loss of these leaders, Pakistan struggled to create a functioning national government. It took a full nine years for its leaders to draft a constitution, a written document outlining how the government would operate.

Pakistan faced numerous other challenges. The nation had a very weak economy. This made it difficult to absorb the millions of poor Muslim refugees entering the country from India. The hostilities between ethnic groups also kept Pakistanis from gaining the sense of national unity they needed to move forward.

East Pakistani forces march through the city of Jessore during the civil war in 1971. At the war's end, East Pakistan became the independent nation of Bangladesh.

In 1958, amid this turmoil, Muhammad Ayub Khan, a general in the Pakistan army, overthrew the government and declared himself president. Under his rule, a new constitution was drafted. It weakened the National Assembly, the government's elected lawmaking body, and granted the president new legislative and economic powers. Following an unsuccessful war with India over Kashmir in 1965, the public lost all confidence in Ayub Khan's rule. He resigned in 1969 in response to protesters demanding a fair presidential election.

Ayub Khan was succeeded by another general, Muhammad Yahya Khan. Yahya Khan held an election, but he was not happy with the results. Bengalis who were elected to the National Assembly pushed for East Pakistan to have more independence from the Pakistani government. When Yahya Khan ignored their demands, the eastern portion of the country tried to secede, or break away, from Pakistan. In 1971, Yahya Khan sent his army into East Pakistan to stop it from seceding. The country was in the midst of a civil war. The military slaughtered more than half a million Bengalis before India intervened. It sent its own troops into East Pakistan and defeated the government forces from West Pakistan. East Pakistan then became the independent nation of Bangladesh.

Changing Leaders

Humiliated by this defeat, Yahya Khan resigned. The military's stranglehold on Pakistan's government loosened as Zulfikar Ali Bhutto, leader of the Pakistan Peoples Party (PPP), became the president and later the prime minister. Bhutto's government adopted a new constitution in 1973. This constitution included a fairer distribution of power.

Civilian rule did not last long, however. Following a disputed election, General Muhammad Zia-ul-Haq seized power in 1977. Zia had Bhutto tried for complicity in the attempted murder of another politician. Bhutto was convicted and hanged.

Muhammad Zia-ul-Haq installed himself as president in 1978. He remained in power until his death in 1988.

Zia suspended the new constitution and reestablished a government run by the military. The general's regime supported a very strict and conservative interpretation of Islam. For instance, people could be sent to prison for eating anything during the daylight hours of Ramadan, the month of the Islamic calendar during which Muslims are expected to fast. Zia was propped up by foreign aid from the United States, Saudi Arabia, and other countries. These nations wanted Pakistan's help in fighting troops from the Soviet Union, which had invaded Afghanistan in 1979.

Zia died in a suspicious plane crash in August 1988. Three months later, Benazir Bhutto, the daughter of the former leader Zulfikar Ali Bhutto, became prime minister. She was

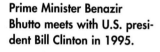

Prime Minister Benazir Bhutto meets with U.S. president Bill Clinton in 1995.

the first woman to lead a modern Muslim nation. For the next eleven years, Bhutto battled her political rivals for control of Pakistan. This period ended in 1999 when another general, Pervez Musharraf, staged a military coup.

Musharraf was the fourth military ruler of Pakistan. Unlike Zia, he largely opposed Islamic extremists and claimed that he wanted to restore economic stability and democracy. But like Zia, Musharraf was kept in power in part because of money given to him by the United States. In 2001, the United States invaded Afghanistan because Afghanistan had been providing shelter to the Islamic extremists who were responsible for the terrorist attacks of September 11, 2001, which had killed nearly three thousand people in the United States. Although Pakistan had supported the Afghan government in the past, it became an American ally. Pakistan decided to accept U.S. aid in return for helping Americans in the Afghan conflict.

Pervez Musharraf and U.S. president George W. Bush answer questions at a 2006 press conference. Pakistan supported the United States in its war in Afghanistan.

Finding Bin Laden

In early May 2011, U.S. commandos staged a raid on a compound in the town of Abbottabad in northern Pakistan. There, they discovered and killed Osama bin Laden—the terrorist leader behind the attacks of September 11, 2001, in New York City, near Washington, D.C., and over Pennsylvania. American intelligence agents had found out that bin Laden had been living there for five years.

The incident put a great strain on U.S.-Pakistani relations. Pakistan was outraged that the United States had approved a military operation in Pakistan without the consent of the Pakistani government. The United States was angry that Pakistan, officially an American ally, had not alerted the U.S. military of bin

Laden's location. Some American officials believe that Pakistan's army or intelligence service knew all along where bin Laden was hiding.

An Uncertain Future

By 2007, many Pakistanis were tired of Musharraf's rule. They were angry that he had not restored democracy as promised. Tensions grew worse when Benazir Bhutto, after living in exile, returned to Pakistan and was assassinated. When Musharraf tried to fire Iftikhar Chaudhry, the chief justice of Pakistan's Supreme Court, Musharraf's opponents took to the streets in protest. After a 2008 election voted Musharraf's supporters out of power, he resigned under pressure. Asif Ali Zardari, Bhutto's widower, became president.

The new regime must deal with some of the same problems that Pakistan faced when it was founded more than sixty years ago. The government remains unstable and the economy weak. The ethnic tensions among the Pakistanis still simmer.

The hostilities between Pakistan and India remain heated. But many things have changed since Partition. Both countries now have nuclear weapons, raising fears that any future conflict between them could be catastrophic.

In recent years, natural disasters have only worsened Pakistan's troubles. In 2005, an earthquake devastated Kashmir, killing an estimated seventy-five thousand people. Then, in 2010, many Pakistanis lost their lives or livelihoods in massive flooding in the Indus River valley. Despite their many difficulties, however, Pakistanis maintain hope that their homeland will soon see better days.

Rescue workers search for survivors in a collapsed apartment building in Islamabad following the 2005 earthquake. The quake forced three million people across South Asia from their homes.

Governing Pakistan

I N 1973, Pakistan's most recent constitution was drafted. Pakistan is a republic, in which the people elect their governmental representatives. But military leaders sometimes overthrow the government when they believe elected officials are taking the country down the wrong path. When this happens, the constitution is suspended, and the legislature is dissolved. Pakistan has continued to be unstable as military governments try to create a democracy that suits their interests.

Opposite: **Sehba Musharraf, the wife of then-president Pervez Musharraf, votes in an election in 2008. Pakistani women received the right to vote in 1956.**

The Legislative Branch

The constitution of Pakistan calls for three branches of government—the legislative, the executive, and the judicial. The legislative branch is made up of the Majlis-e-Shoora, which means "council of advisers" in Urdu. The Majlis-e-Shoora is a parliament (lawmaking body) with two houses.

The Flag of Pakistan

Just days before it became an independent country, Pakistan adopted its national flag. Modeled on the flag of the All-India Muslim League, it consists of two sections—a white vertical stripe on the left side and a large green field on the right. In the center of the green field is a white crescent and five-pointed star. The green section represents the nation's Muslim majority, while the white stripe symbolizes the religious minorities living within its borders. The crescent stands for progress, and the star represents knowledge and light.

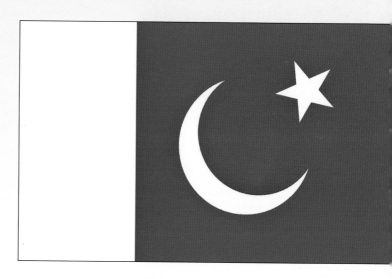

The larger house is the National Assembly. In 2011, it had 342 members. Voters elect assembly members to five-year terms. (Citizens at least eighteen years old can vote in Pakistan.)

Yousaf Raza Gilani, who was prime minister until 2012, speaks to the National Assembly.

Pakistan's National Government

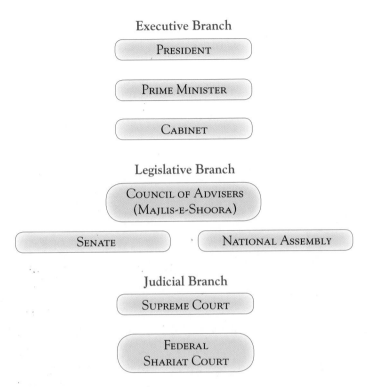

Executive Branch

> PRESIDENT

> PRIME MINISTER

> CABINET

Legislative Branch

> COUNCIL OF ADVISERS
> (MAJLIS-E-SHOORA)

> SENATE

> NATIONAL ASSEMBLY

Judicial Branch

> SUPREME COURT

> FEDERAL
> SHARIAT COURT

Sixty seats are reserved for women, and 10 are designated for non-Muslims. According to the constitution, non-Muslim legislators have to be educated in Islam and its principles.

The smaller legislative house is the Senate, with 104 members. Representatives in the National Assembly elect senators to six-year terms. In the Senate, 17 seats must be held by women and 4 by people from religious minorities.

The legislatures of Pakistan's four provinces—Punjab, Balochistan, Sindh, and Khyber Pakhtunkhwa—each send 14 representatives to the Senate. These provinces are political divisions that function similarly to states within the United States. Areas in Pakistan that are not formally part of the provinces are also represented in the Senate. They include the Islamabad Capital Territory in the national capital of Islamabad and the thirteen Federally Administered Tribal Areas. These areas are located in the west between Balochistan, Khyber Pakhtunkhwa, and the international border with Afghanistan.

Each province in Pakistan has its own legislature to handle regional issues. The Sindh Province assembly meets in Karachi.

The New Capital

In 1959, Pakistan's government decided to move its capital out of Karachi, Pakistan's largest city. The next year, officials chose a site in northeastern Pakistan for the new capital. This site was easy to reach from all areas of the country. After a massive building effort, the glittering modern city of Islamabad became the seat of Pakistan's national government. Many of its buildings, including landmarks such as the Faisal Mosque (right) and the Pakistan Monument, combine contemporary and traditional Islamic architectural styles.

The carefully planned layout of Islamabad contains eight zones, including educational, industrial, and diplomatic districts. Each zone has its own shopping area and park. Highways connect the capital to the city of Rawalpindi, which lies only 9 miles (15 km) away. Rawalpindi, the fourth-largest city in Pakistan, is Islamabad's sister city. An estimated 832,000 people live in Islamabad, but the Rawalpindi-Islamabad metropolitan area has a population of approximately 4.5 million.

In recent years, Islamabad has suffered greatly. An earthquake hit in 2005, and the city has been struck by many terrorist attacks. Despite its struggles, Islamabad remains Pakistan's most modern and cosmopolitan urban area.

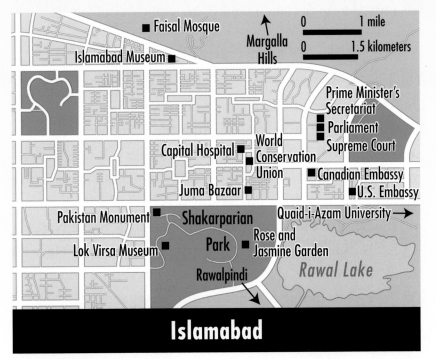

Islamabad

President Asif Ali Zardari meets with children forced from their homes by a flood. Zardari became president in 2008.

Both of the houses of the Majlis-e-Shoora meet at the Parliament House in Islamabad. Each house may pass laws, but only the National Assembly can approve budgets.

The Executive Branch

The highest officials in the executive branch are the president and the prime minister. The president is the head of state and has mainly ceremonial duties, while the prime minister is the head of the government. The prime minister oversees the government's day-to-day operations. This system is different from the U.S. system, where the president is both the head of state and the head of the government. The members of the National Assembly, the Senate, and the provincial legislatures elect the president. Presidential candidates must be Muslim and at least forty-five years old. Presidents serve a five-year term.

The president formally appoints the prime minister, who has to be a member of the National Assembly. Generally, the prime minister is the leader of the political party with the most assembly seats. The prime minister is assisted by a cabinet (or council) of ministers, which heads various departments in the national government. Each department deals with a specific concern, such as defense, education, railways, health, housing, and youth affairs. The president appoints the cabinet ministers after getting recommendations from the prime minister.

The Judicial Branch

The Supreme Court is the highest court in Pakistan. It has the power to overturn laws that it determines are unconstitutional. A chief justice, who is appointed by the president, heads the court.

Since Pakistan was once part of British-controlled India, Pakistani law is related to British law. But it is also influenced by Islamic law derived from the Qur'an, the holy book of

Supreme Court justices enter a courtroom.

General and President

Pervez Musharraf, Pakistan's longtime military dictator, was born in New Delhi, India, in 1943. He moved with his family to Karachi in the newly created nation of Pakistan in 1947. As a young man, Musharraf attended the Pakistan Military Academy. He fought in Pakistan's brief war with India in 1965 and was involved in the 1971 civil war, during which Bangladesh (formerly East Pakistan) declared independence.

Musharraf rose to the rank of general and in 1998 became the head of Pakistan's Joint Chiefs of Staff under Prime Minister Nawaz Sharif. However, at one point when Musharraf was out of the country, Sharif attempted to dismiss him from his position. With the support of other military leaders, Musharraf ousted the prime minister and took over the Pakistani government in October 1999.

Musharraf helped solidify his control over the country by becoming an ally of the United States. After the terrorist attacks of September 11, 2001, the U.S. government sought to destroy the Taliban, an Islamic radical group that controlled the government of Afghanistan. By helping the United States in its war in Afghanistan, Musharraf was able to secure U.S. aid to help prop up Pakistan's ailing economy. Musharraf's position, however, put him in conflict with Islamic militants within Pakistan.

Musharraf's regime was also challenged in 2007, when he attempted to oust the chief justice of the Supreme Court. Protesters took to the streets to denounce Musharraf, who responded by imposing military rule and rounding up his political opponents. After his party lost a 2008 national election, Musharraf chose to resign from office.

Musharraf moved to England, but he remains involved in Pakistani politics. In 2010, he created a new political party, the All Pakistan Muslim League.

Islam. To make sure that all laws were consistent with the teachings of Islam, Pakistan established the Federal Shariat Court. The court is made up of eight justices, three of whom are *ulama*, or scholars of Muslim law. The Council of Islamic Ideology helps legislators determine whether a law they are considering violates Islamic principles in any way.

In the Pakistani legal system, below the Supreme Court are provincial high courts and other lower courts that hear criminal and civil cases. This formal justice system has little control over the tribal Pashtun people who live in western Pakistan. Disputes there are commonly settled by tribal leaders, based on a traditional system of laws called the Pakhtunwali. This system has been in force for centuries. Some tribal leaders even have their own private prisons to punish wrongdoers.

The Supreme Court meets in Islamabad.

"Qaumi Tarana"

Soon after Pakistan became an independent country, its new government established the National Anthem Committee. The group considered many songs before choosing one written by well-known composer Ahmed G. Chagla as Pakistan's national anthem. The committee invited prominent poets to write lyrics for the anthem. After selecting the Urdu lyrics written by Abul Asar Hafeez Jullundhri, the government officially adopted "Qaumi Tarana" as Pakistan's anthem in 1954. The song's official title means "national anthem." But many people refer to it by its first line, "Pak sarzamin shad bad," or "Blessed be the sacred land." The anthem is frequently sung on patriotic national holidays, such as Pakistan Day and Independence Day.

English translation

Blessed be the sacred land,
Happy be the bounteous realm,
Symbol of high resolve,
Land of Pakistan.
Blessed be thou citadel of faith.

The Order of this Sacred Land
Is the might of the brotherhood of the people.
May the nation, the country, and the State
Shine in glory everlasting.
Blessed be the goal of our ambition.

This flag of the Crescent and the Star
Leads the way to progress and perfection,
Interpreter of our past, glory of our present,
Inspiration of our future,
Symbol of Almighty's protection.

Politics in Practice

Like the government of the United States, the government of Pakistan was designed with a system of checks and balances to prevent any one branch from becoming too powerful. But many times in Pakistan's short history, leaders have disregarded their constitution in order to amass more power for themselves. Since 1947, the country has often been under the rule of dictators who gained control over the government, not through legitimate elections, but through assassinations and military takeovers.

A soldier patrols in Karachi. The military has played a major role in the history and government of Pakistan.

Although the executive branch is supposed to share power with the legislative and the judicial branches, military leaders have routinely weakened the other branches of government. For instance, the last military leader, Pervez Musharraf, disbanded the National Assembly and tried to dismiss the chief justice of the Supreme Court. The constitution of Pakistan guarantees certain freedoms to its citizens, such as freedom of speech and freedom of the press. But in times of military rule, these rights had little meaning, as the army worked to suppress and silence any critics of the regime.

Benazir Bhutto

In 1988, Benazir Bhutto became the first female prime minister of Pakistan, making her the first woman to lead a modern Muslim nation. Bhutto was born on June 21, 1953, into a prominent political family. Her father, Zulfikar Ali Bhutto, had served as president and prime minister of Pakistan in the 1970s. He was ousted from power in 1977 in a military coup led by General Muhammad Zia-ul-Haq, who later had Bhutto's father executed.

A graduate of Radcliffe College in the United States and University of Oxford in England, Bhutto became a leader in the Pakistan Peoples Party (PPP), a political party her father founded. Because of her opposition to Zia, she was repeatedly arrested. She eventually fled to England, where she continued her political activities in exile. In 1985, military rule and political party bans were ended, leading to Bhutto's return to Pakistan in

1986. Following the death of Zia, a general election was held in November 1988. The PPP won a majority of seats in the National Assembly, and Bhutto became prime minister. She served in this post from 1988 to 1990 and from 1993 to 1996. Bhutto struggled in her efforts to reform Pakistan's government, especially after numerous corruption charges were leveled at her and her husband, Asif Ali Zardari (above, left).

In 1999, the military once again took control of Pakistan. Bhutto left the country, returning in 2007 only after President Pervez Musharraf, under popular pressure, granted her amnesty. While campaigning with a pro-democracy platform, she was assassinated at a PPP rally on December 27, 2007. The next year the PPP, now led by Bhutto's widower, won the national elections. After Musharraf was forced from power in late 2008, Zardari became the president of Pakistan.

Even when Pakistanis have been permitted to freely elect their leaders, power still often remains in the hands of only a select few. In remote areas of the country, for instance, people rarely receive services from the national government. They instead rely on wealthy local leaders for aid and support. Understandably, people tend to vote for these local leaders, which means only the most privileged have a role in the government. But increasingly, younger, less affluent people are insisting that they have a voice as well. In the years to come, they may help lead Pakistan toward a fairer and more just form of government than the country has seen in the past.

A young woman displays her identification in a polling place. On average, only 42 percent of Pakistanis who can vote actually go to the polls. This is one of the lowest voting rates in the world.

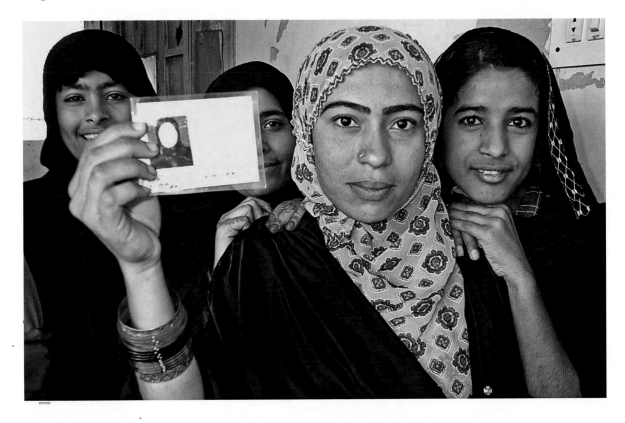

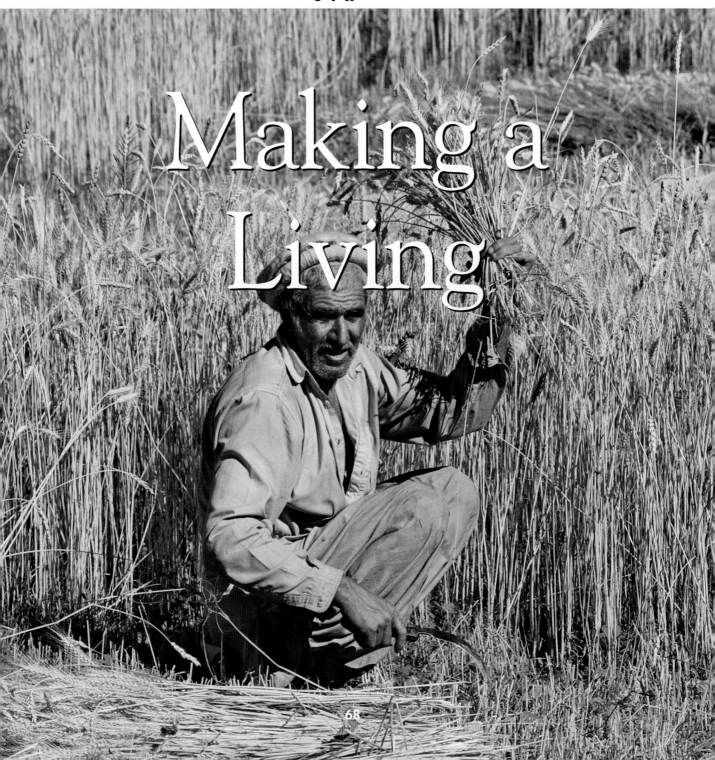

Making a Living

ONE OF PAKISTAN'S GREATEST PROBLEMS IS SLOW economic growth. Because of its history of political troubles and the instability of its government, few foreign investors want to put money into businesses in Pakistan. The national government spends a large percentage of its money on the military, so it does not have enough left over to put into economic development.

There are some bright spots in Pakistan's economic picture, though. Poverty rates are dropping, and as years go by, more and more Pakistanis are earning enough to be considered middle class. But many workers must still struggle to survive on meager wages. Finding a job can be hard. The official unemployment rate in 2010 was about 15 percent, but the real rate was probably higher. Adding to workers' woes, inflation—the rate at which prices for goods rise—is high. As a result of inflation, the little money most Pakistanis earn purchases less than it once did.

Opposite: **A man in northern Pakistan harvests wheat, one of the nation's most important crops. The vast majority of Pakistani wheat is used within the country rather than exported.**

The Metric System

Pakistan's official system of weights and measures is the metric system.

Metric measures of distance
1 centimeter = 0.39 inches
1 meter = 3.28 feet
1 kilometer = 0.62 miles

Metric measures of volume
1 liter = 1.06 quarts

Metric measures of weight
1 kilogram = 2.20 pounds

Four in every ten Pakistani workers make a living from farming. Agriculture accounts for about 22 percent of Pakistan's gross domestic product (GDP), the total goods and services the country produces each year.

Most of the country's farmland is concentrated in the Punjab and Sindh provinces along the Indus River and its tributaries. However, much of this farmland has to be irrigated for crops to flourish. The most important food crops grown in Pakistan are wheat, rice, and sugarcane. Fruits and vegetables—including onions, apricots, dates, mangoes, oranges, and tangerines—are also a large part of the agricultural economy. Cotton is the most lucrative cash crop. The cotton grown in Pakistan fuels the country's large textile industry.

A Pakistani woman picks cotton. Pakistan is the world's fourth-largest cotton producer.

Cotton cloth, clothing, bed sheets, and yarn are some of Pakistan's leading export products.

Many farmers also raise livestock, including chickens for their eggs and cattle and sheep for their meat. Sheep are kept and sheared for their wool, which is used to make yarn.

Pakistan's fishing industry is based along the coast near Karachi. Much of the fish, lobster, and shrimp caught there is exported to other countries.

Industry and Services

When Pakistan was founded in 1947, industry was just a tiny part of its economy. Since then, Pakistani industry has been growing by leaps and bounds. Textiles are the biggest industry

Pakistani fishers throw their catch into a donkey cart to be taken to market.

A worker places labels on cricket bats at a factory in Sialkot.

in the country. Textiles produced include cotton cloth, carpets, and rugs. Increasingly, the country's factories manufacture a wide variety of other goods as well. Chemicals, processed food, fertilizer, sugar, construction materials, paper products, medicines, and leather goods are all made in Pakistan. The city of Sialkot in Punjab Province produces many surgical instruments and sporting goods, including hand-sewn footballs that are used in international competitions. In total, manufacturing makes up about 24 percent of Pakistan's GDP.

The largest part of the nation's economy is the service sector, which employs more than 40 percent of Pakistani workers. Service workers sell goods or provide services for customers. Top service industries in Pakistan include banking, transportation, and retail sales.

Ending Pakistani Child Labor

Pakistan's factories employ millions of children, some as young as four years old. Although child labor is against the law, many employees hire children from poor families because they can pay them an extremely low wage. Child workers are especially common in the carpet-making business because, by the nature of having small fingers, children can pull yarn into tiny knots much more easily than large-fingered adults can. The children often work long hours in dirty and uncomfortable conditions. Because they are working full-time, they usually have no opportunity to go to school.

Activists all over the world are working to end child labor in Pakistan. Many people have been inspired by the life of Iqbal Masih (left). He was a Pakistani boy who was sold into slavery to a carpet weaver when he was four years old. When Iqbal was twelve, he escaped from his employer and began speaking out against child labor. His story drew international attention. However, Iqbal's life and work were cut short when, in 1995, at thirteen, he was murdered by a gun blast while he was riding his bike home. His murderer was never caught. Since 2009, the U.S. Department of Labor has presented the annual Iqbal Masih Award to a person, organization, or government dedicated to stopping child labor and slavery.

Tourism is a small but growing service industry. Mountain climbers and hikers are attracted to the hills and mountains of northern Pakistan. Many Pakistanis from the southern plains also visit the north during the summer to escape the heat. Both

Miners use a trolley to leave a coal mine in southern Pakistan.

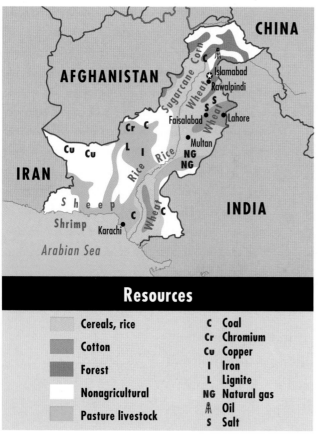

CHINA

AFGHANISTAN

IRAN

INDIA

Islamabad
Rawalpindi
Faisalabad
Lahore
Multan
Karachi

Sugarcane
Corn
Wheat
Wheat
Rice
Rice
Wheat
Sheep
Shrimp
Arabian Sea

Cr
C
Cu
Cu
L
I
NG
NG
C
C

Resources

Cereals, rice		C	Coal
Cotton		Cr	Chromium
Forest		Cu	Copper
		I	Iron
Nonagricultural		L	Lignite
		NG	Natural gas
Pasture livestock			Oil
		S	Salt

Pakistani and foreign vacationers enjoy the attractions of large cities, such as the nightlife of Karachi and the architectural wonders of Lahore. Tourism, however, has yet to truly take off in Pakistan because the nation's unstable political situation keeps away many potential visitors.

Mining and Energy

Mining is only a small part of the Pakistani economy. Today, only about one Pakistani laborer out of one thousand works in the mining industry. But the country has deposits of dozens of minerals including iron, copper, gypsum, and chromite.

Coal has also long been mined in Pakistan. Its quality is poor, however, so there is little demand for it. Oil deposits recently discovered in the Sindh province have the potential for boosting the national economy someday.

Pakistan's own demands for energy have increased greatly in recent years. More energy sources are needed to fuel both factories and homes. In addition, as the population rises and more Pakistanis move to cities, there is a greater demand than ever for reliable electricity. The government has tried to meet these needs by promoting solar energy, which turns sunlight

What Pakistan Grows, Makes, and Mines

Agriculture (2011)

Wheat	24,000,000 metric tons
Rice	6,650,000 metric tons
Cotton	10,000,000 bales (480 pounds [218 kg] each)

Industry (2006, in value added by manufacturing)

Textiles	US$4,241,000,000
Food products	US$2,527,000,000
Chemical products	US$2,124,000,000

Mining

Iron ore (2009)	135,000 metric tons
Copper (2008)	18,700 metric tons
Gypsum (2008)	640,000 metric tons

A salesperson cleans off his solar panels. The Pakistani government is encouraging the use of solar power.

into electricity, and hydroelectric power, which uses running water to create electricity. At the same time, the government is discouraging people in rural areas from using firewood for fuel, in order to protect the northern forests.

Getting Around

Another obstacle to Pakistan's economic growth is its transportation system. The government has been slow to fund transportation projects and repairs, so its present system doesn't always meet the needs of its large population.

Pakistani Truck Art

The busy streets of Pakistan almost seem like an art gallery. But the art on display isn't in frames on a wall. It's on the sides of the trucks and buses that carry goods and passengers from place to place in the nation's cities.

Decades ago, bus companies hoped to attract customers by painting logos on the vehicles. As time went by, bus and truck decorations became more elaborate. Once confined to paint and wood, they now often incorporate metal, tinsel, plastic, reflective tape, mirrors, and sometimes even lighting systems.

Frequently, every inch of a vehicle is adorned with designs and images in bright purple, red, green, and yellow. The decorations on the front of a truck are usually more serious. They might incorporate religious symbols or verses from the Qur'an. The backs of the trucks feature more whimsical artwork. For example, they might depict peaceful landscapes or portraits of film stars or other celebrities.

Drivers are very proud of their decorated trucks. They often devote the equivalent of thousands of dollars to adorning their vehicles. Truck decoration is a big business in Pakistan's cities. In Karachi alone, there are about fifty thousand artisans who make a living adorning vehicles to owners' precise specifications.

For long-distance travel, trains are the best option. Pakistan has about 8,000 miles (13,000 km) of train tracks, but many need repair. Trains tend to be crowded, uncomfortable, and unreliable.

Pakistan has some 150 airfields, about two-thirds of which have paved runways. The largest is Jinnah International Airport in Karachi, which serves six million passengers a year. Passengers can travel to international locations from Karachi and other major cities, such as Lahore and Rawalpindi. The country's biggest air carrier is Pakistan International Airlines, which is owned by the Pakistani government.

For day-to-day travel in cities, many Pakistanis rely on buses and taxis, because few people can afford their own cars. In the past, people could cover short distances in *tongas* (horse-drawn carriages), but increasingly these have been replaced by motorized rickshaws.

Building a Better Economy

In the early twenty-first century, the economy of Pakistan was improving, in part because of funds provided by its most

Money Facts

The unit of currency in Pakistan is the rupee. Coins come in values of 1, 2, and 5 rupees. Paper money has values of 5, 10, 20, 50, 100, 500, 1,000, and 5,000 rupees. All bills have a picture of Mohammed Ali Jinnah, the founder of Pakistan on the front. On the reverse of the paper bills are prominent buildings and natural wonders in Pakistan. For example, the 20-rupee note shows the ruins of the ancient city of Mohenjo Daro, and the 50-rupee note depicts K2, the second-highest mountain in the world. In 2012, US$1.00 equaled about 90 rupees.

important political ally, the United States. But an earthquake in 2005, a worldwide economic downturn in 2008, and extensive flooding in 2010 brought that growth to a standstill.

Improving Pakistan's economy over the long-term is a huge challenge. To get the needed revenue for economic investment and development, the government will have to make substantial reforms. Many Pakistanis have taken to the streets demanding just these changes. They want an end to government corruption, an increase in educational opportunities, improved electricity production, and better management of Pakistan's natural resources. They hope that if the government makes changes such as these, Pakistan may one day become a more prosperous place for all its citizens.

In 2011, Pakistanis took to the streets to protest rising prices and government corruption.

CHAPTER

SEVEN

The Pakistani People

M ORE THAN 190 MILLION PEOPLE LIVE IN Pakistan, making it the sixth most populated nation in the world. The people are not spread evenly throughout the country, however. Some areas are largely empty of people because of extreme terrains or climate. Most Pakistanis live in the hospitable regions of Punjab and Sindh. These provinces are home to nearly 79 percent of all Pakistanis.

The population of Pakistan is very young compared to most countries. The median age is about twenty-two. More than one-third of all Pakistanis are under fifteen years old, while only 4 percent are sixty-five or older.

Opposite: **Children playing in Karachi**

Punjabis

The Pakistani population is extraordinarily diverse. Its people belong to many different ethnic groups that are defined by language, customs, and geography. Three of the four Pakistani provinces are named after ethnic groups found in the country.

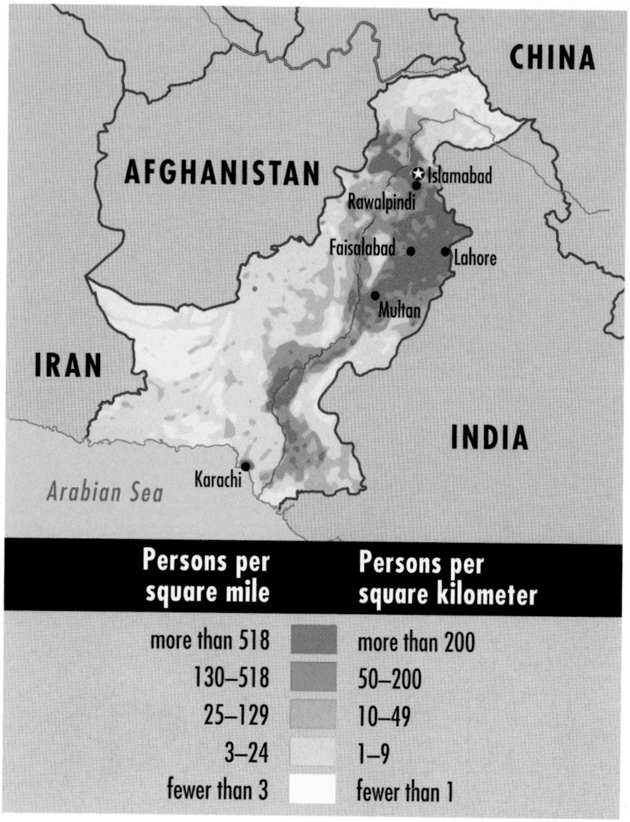
CHINA
AFGHANISTAN
Islamabad
Rawalpindi
Faisalabad
Lahore
Multan
IRAN
INDIA
Karachi
Arabian Sea
Persons per square mile
Persons per square kilometer
more than 518
more than 200
130–518
50–200
25–129
10–49
3–24
1–9
fewer than 3
fewer than 1

About 45 percent of Pakistanis are Punjabi. Most of them live in the province of Punjab, which means "land of five rivers," and in the Pakistani-administered area of Kashmir. A smaller population of Punjabis lives in India in a state also named Punjab.

Traditionally, Punjabis were farmers and artisans. Today, many Punjabis work for the government, particularly the military. They are the most economically successful and politically influential ethnic group in the country.

Pashtuns and Sindhis

The second-largest ethnic group in Pakistan, making up about 15 percent of the population, is the Pashtun. They mostly live in the Khyber Pakhtunkhwa, a province that was called the North-West Frontier before 2010. Pashtuns pushed for the name change, because Pakhtunkhwa has long been their name for their homeland.

Pashtuns have traditionally been tribal people who made their living as farmers and shepherds. Their many tribes include the Afridi, Khattak, Waziri, and Yusufzai. Pashtuns initially opposed the creation of Pakistan because the international border with Afghanistan separated them from their Pashtun kinsmen in that country. Until recently, many Pashtuns have felt more allegiance

Ethnic Groups in Pakistan

Punjabi	45%
Pashtun	15%
Sindhi	14%
Saraiki	8%
Muhajir	8%
Balochi	4%
Other	6%

to Pakhtunkhwa than to Pakistan. But as they have gained power in the national government, they have become more invested in the country. At the same time, some Pashtuns have moved to places in Pakistan outside of Khyber Pakhtunkhwa. There is now a large community of Pashtuns living in Karachi.

The next largest Pakistani ethnic group is the Sindhi. As their name suggests, they are the dominant group in the province of Sindh. Their language, also called Sindhi, is similar to Punjabi. Traditionally hunters, they have increasingly found work in agriculture.

Pashtun men in Peshawar. Pashtuns are the second-largest ethnic group in Pakistan.

Population of the Largest Cities (2010 est.)

Karachi	13,205,339
Lahore	7,129,609
Faisalabad	2,990,675
Rawalpindi	1,409,768
Multan	1,197,384

Most Sindhi people live in southeastern Pakistan.

Other Ethnic Groups

Another ethnic group with an important place in Pakistani history is the Muhajir. They are the descendants of Muslim refugees from central and southern India who moved to Pakistan in the years after it was partitioned from India. The Muhajir is the only group in Pakistan that speaks Urdu.

Muhajirs largely settled in the Sindh province, particularly in its capital of Karachi, the country's center for business and industry. There, they established family-run businesses and lived in large houses filled with relatives. Muhajirs quickly outnumbered the Sindhi population in the region. Struggling

for control over Sindh, the Muhajirs and Sindhis have often come into conflict, sometimes resulting in violence.

Balochis make up just shy of 4 percent of the Pakistani population. They live in the rugged mountains and valleys of the Balochistan province. Some Balochis have wanted to secede from Pakistan just as the Bengalis did in 1971. However, their desires for their own country were quashed during bloody fighting with the Pakistani army.

Other Pakistani ethnic groups include the Saraiki, who live mostly in Punjab, and the Brahi, who are found in Sindh and Balochistan. The country is also home to small numbers of other groups, such as the Gujrati, Chitrali, and Kashmiri.

Balochi girls in southern Pakistan. They are wearing traditional embroidered headscarves.

Speaking Urdu

Kya haal hae?	How are you?
T'heek hoon	I am fine
Assalam aléikum	God's peace be with you (greeting)
Wa'al éikum salam	And with you too (response to greeting)
Khodáh hafíz	God be with you (good-bye)
Shúkri'a	Thank you
Bóhat shúkri'a	Thank you very much

Pakistani Languages

Pakistanis are separated not only by ethnicity, but also by language. Punjabi is the first language of roughly half the Pakistani people. But many other languages are also heard in the country. Pashtuns speak dialects of the Pashto language. Sindhis speak Sindhi, and Balochis speak Balochi. Smaller groups speak more obscure languages, including Hindko, Brahui, and Persian.

But none of these are Pakistan's official language. That honor falls to Urdu. It is the first language of about 8 percent of Pakistanis, including many Muhajirs.

Unlike most languages spoken in Pakistan, Urdu is fairly modern. It was created during the period when the

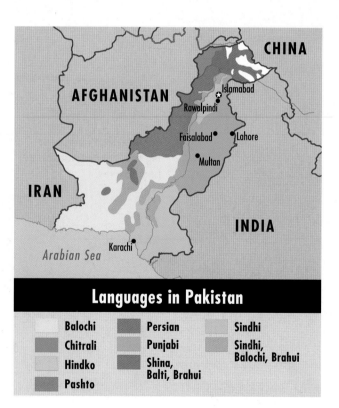

Languages in Pakistan

Balochi	Persian	Sindhi	
Chitrali	Punjabi	Sindhi, Balochi, Brahui	
Hindko	Shina, Balti, Brahui		
Pashto			

Mughal Empire ruled the region that is present-day Pakistan. The empire's soldiers did not know the languages of the local populations. To help them communicate with the Mughal subjects, Urdu was invented. It combined words from Hindi, Persian, and Arabic, so people from many different linguistic backgrounds could quickly learn to speak and understand it.

A man paints religious verses in Urdu on a wall in Karachi.

Children studying Urdu. About 45 percent of Pakistani women and 69 percent of Pakistani men can read and write.

The government of Pakistan adopted Urdu in the hope that it could similarly bring together all the different peoples of the country. But outside of the Muhajirs, Urdu is spoken mainly by the educated class. Young Pakistanis who are lucky enough to attend school are eager to learn Urdu because it can help them get jobs with the government.

Over the years, many Pakistanis have objected to Urdu being the official language of their country. They think that it limits the job opportunities of non-Urdu speakers. They also see Urdu's official status as a way of trying to erode their own ethnic identities. Some people have worked to change the government's policy, but for now Urdu remains the official language of Pakistan, if not the one most commonly heard.

English is also a useful language for Pakistanis to know. Many people want to learn it because it can aid them in gov-

The Urdu Alphabet

The Urdu language is written using an alphabet similar to that used to write Persian. It includes thirty-eight characters, which are written and read from right to left. The letters are often joined together in a script style called Nastaliq. It was supposedly first developed in the fourteenth century by a calligrapher named Mir Ali Tabrizi, in what is now Iran. Nastaliq is also used to write Arabic, Persian, and other languages.

Urdu can also be written with the Latin alphabet used to write English. Many young Pakistanis are using the Latin alphabet to send text messages in Urdu.

ernment and business dealings in Pakistan and other parts of the world. People in cities are much more likely to speak English than people in rural areas. In fact, most city dwellers, even the uneducated, know at least a few words of English.

Several English-language newspapers are published in Karachi, including the *Daily News.*

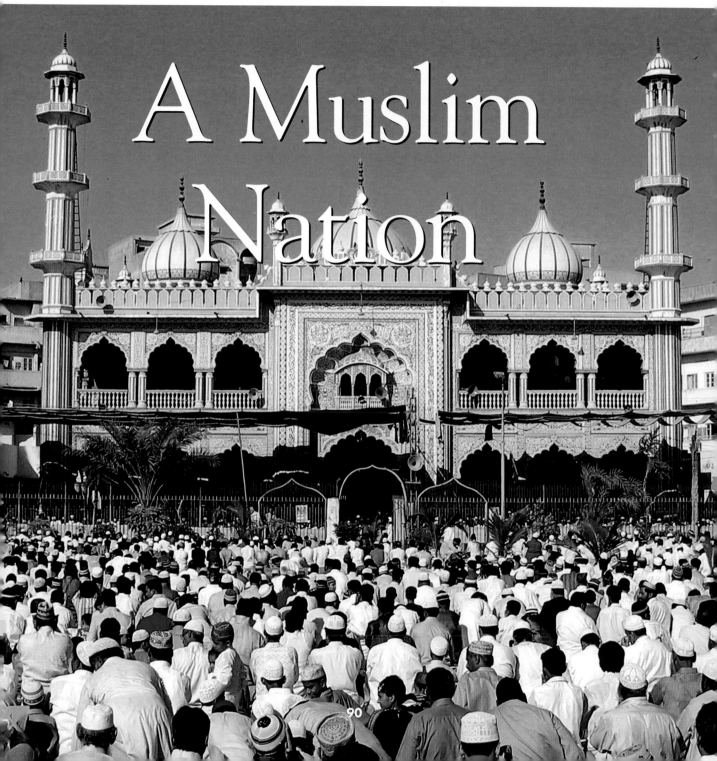

A Muslim Nation

D ESPITE THEIR MANY DIFFERENCES, NEARLY ALL Pakistanis have one thing in common—Islam. About 177,975,600 Pakistanis—95 percent of the population—are Muslims. Around the globe, there are more than 1.5 billion Muslims, making Islam the second most common religion in the world, after Christianity.

The Origins of Islam

Islam was introduced in the eighth century into the area that is now Pakistan. It was the religion of the Arab forces led by Muhammad bin Qasim, which invaded and conquered the Sindh region in 711 CE. Subsequent Muslim rulers extended Islam's influence throughout Pakistan and northern India.

Islam had its origins in the city of Mecca in what is now Saudi Arabia. Muhammad was born there around 570 CE. According to Muslim beliefs, when Muhammad was about forty

Religious Minorities

Only 5 percent of Pakistanis are not Muslims. One of the largest religious minorities is the Hindus. Most Hindus who once lived in Pakistan moved to India when Pakistan was created in 1947, but about three million remain. The majority lives in the Sindh province. About three million Christians also live in Pakistan. Most make their homes in Punjab, although there is a community of Roman Catholics in Karachi. Other religions practiced by a fairly small number of Pakistanis include Sikhism, Zoroastrianism, and Bahaism.

years old, the angel Gabriel visited him. Gabriel passed on to him messages from God, which is "Allah" in Arabic. This is the same God as the one Jews and Christians believe in. These messages explained how to worship God and how to live a proper life. Muhammad began to speak about these messages and soon

Muslims always pray facing toward Mecca, Saudi Arabia, the holiest city in Islam.

had many followers. His followers collected into the Qur'an, the holy book of Islam, the revelations Muhammad received from Gabriel. Many figures mentioned in the Qur'an, such as Noah, Jesus, and Mary, also appear in the Bible.

Officials in Mecca were suspicious of Muhammad, whom they believed might challenge their power. Fearing that he might be killed, Muhammad fled Mecca for Medina, another city in what is now Saudi Arabia. This journey became known as the Hijrah. After the death of Muhammad in 632, Islam continued to spread. It is now the dominant religion in much of northern Africa and southwestern Asia.

An ancient Qur'an in the Lahore Museum. The verses of the Qur'an are said to be the direct messages God sent to Muhammad.

Religion in Pakistan

Muslim	95%
Sunni	75%
Shi'i	20%
Other (includes Christian and Hindu)	5%

The Five Pillars of Islam

Muslims in Pakistan and elsewhere are supposed to perform certain religious duties known as the Five Pillars of Islam.

The first, *shahadah*, calls on Muslims to affirm their belief in Islam by saying, "There is no God but God and Muhammad is the messenger of God." The second, *salah*, says that Muslims should pray five times a day, at dawn, noon, afternoon, sunset, and evening. Each time, they bow and kneel so that their bodies are facing Mecca, the holy city where the Prophet Muhammad was born. Many Muslims structure their daily lives around these prayers. *Zakat* is the third pillar. It requires Muslims to offer money to the poor. The fourth pillar, *sawm*, obliges Muslims to fast, or not eat, from sunup to sundown every day during the holy month of Ramadan. The fifth pillar is *hajj*. This pillar requires all Muslims to visit Mecca at least once in their lives if they are physically and financially able to.

Sunnis, Shi'is, and Ahmadis

Over time, Islam has divided into different sects, or versions. There are differences in how each sect practices Islam.

The main sects are Sunni and Shi'i. After the death of Muhammad, these two groups disagreed over who should be the caliph, or leader, of Islam. The Sunnis thought that the successor should be selected from a group of elite Muslims. The Shi'is wanted the caliph to be a direct descendant of Muhammad.

Around the world today, the majority of Muslims are Sunni. In Pakistan, Sunnis make up about 75 percent of the population. Some 20 percent of Pakistanis are Shi'is. Throughout Pakistan's history, friction has existed between these two groups. This friction has sometimes erupted into violence.

Another sect, the Ahmadi, also considers itself Muslim. Ahmadis make up a little more than 2 percent of the Pakistani population. The Ahmadis' beliefs grew out of a late nineteenth-century movement in India to revitalize Islam. The Ahmadis hold some views that are controversial among other Muslims, including the belief that Muhammad is not the final prophet and messenger of God. Because of the Ahmadis' beliefs, other Pakistani Muslims have challenged

Every year, more than two million Muslims make a pilgrimage to Mecca, Saudi Arabia.

Members of Pakistan's Ahmadi community mourn those who were killed in an attack in Lahore in 2010.

their commitment to Islam. In 1974, the government changed Pakistan's constitution so that it declared that Ahmadis were officially considered non-Muslims.

The Ahmadis have since faced discrimination and persecution. For instance, they can be sentenced to prison if they enter non-Ahmadi mosques or if they quote the Qur'an in public. The Ahmadis have also been subject to violent attacks. One of the most brutal occurred in May 2010 in Lahore. Radical Sunnis fired guns and lobbed grenades into two Ahmadi mosques, killing ninety-three worshippers.

Holy Celebrations

As a largely Islamic nation, Pakistanis come together each year to celebrate and observe certain religious festivities. The longest such observance is the month of Ramadan. This month commemorates the period during which Muhammad is said to have received messages from God. During Ramadan, Muslims eat nothing during daylight hours. They eat only in the morning before sunrise and at night after sunset. During this holy month, they also try to read the Qur'an more often and spend more time at their mosque.

At the end of Ramadan, Muslims celebrate 'Id al-Fitr. During this happy occasion, people feast on all the foods they missed while fasting. They also visit friends and family. Parents often give children colorful new outfits and other gifts as part of the festivities.

Children dress in their best clothing for 'Id al-Fitr.

The First Ahmadi

Mirza Ghulam Ahmad, the founder of the Ahmadiyya religious movement, was born in 1835 in what is now the city of Qadian, India. Ahmad was a devout Sunni Muslim who wrote a book defending Islam against attacks by Christians. He disputed the Christian belief that Jesus was the Messiah, the promised savior of mankind. Eventually, Ahmad came to believe that he himself was the Messiah and a great prophet of Islam. This claim offended many Muslims and led to the persecution of Ahmad's followers. Ahmad died in Lahore in 1908, but his religious movement lived on. In Pakistan, more than five million people are practicing Ahmadis.

Shi'i Muslims take part in a parade on Ashura.

'Id al-Adha is a more somber religious holiday. It celebrates the obedience of the prophet Ibrahim (called Abraham in the Bible), who, according to the Qur'an, was willing to sacrifice his son when God asked him to. God rewarded Ibrahim by having an animal sacrificed in his son's place. On 'Id al-Adha, Pakistani Muslims reenact this sacrifice by slaughtering a goat, calf, or sheep. Each household offers a portion of the meat to friends, family, and the poor. The hides of the animals are often donated to mosques. The hides are then sold, and the money is given to charity.

Another holy day, particularly for Pakistani Shi'is, is Ashura. This holiday commemorates the murder of al-Husayn ibn Ali, a grandson of Muhammad. Shi'is believe he was the Prophet's rightful successor. During processions on Ashura, some Shi'is beat themselves in order to feel al-Husayn's suffering. Other Muslim holidays celebrated throughout Pakistan include Mawlid, the birthday of Muhammad, and Mi'raj, the anniversary of the Prophet's ascension into heaven. On the night of Mi'raj, Pakistanis light up cities with candles, oil lamps, and electric lights as they pray.

During Ramadan, Muslims eat only when the sun is down. Here, a boy in Islamabad sets out food in preparation for the breaking of the fast after dark.

Religious Holidays

Major Islamic holidays observed annually by Pakistani Muslims include:

Mawlid	Birthday of the Prophet Muhammad
Mi'raj	Muhammad's ascent into heaven
Ramadan	A month of fasting
'Id al-Fitr	Celebration of the end of Ramadan
'Id al-Adha	Commemoration of Ibrahim's willingness to sacrifice his son to God
Ashura	Commemoration of the death of Muhammad's grandson al-Husayn ibn Ali

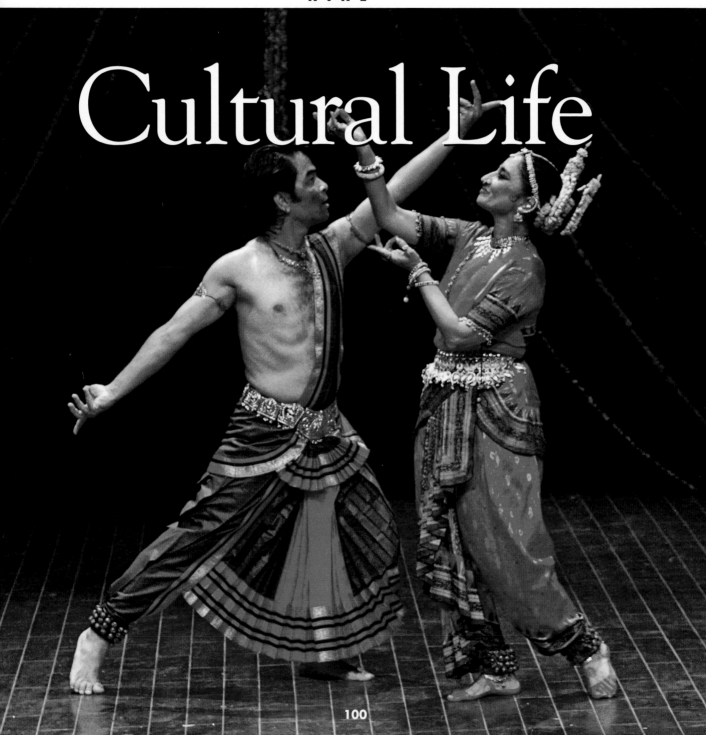

Cultural Life

THE ART AND CULTURE OF PAKISTAN CANNOT BE separated from its history. Over the centuries, Pakistan has been invaded by a series of foreigners. These invaders left a mark on the lives of the people of Pakistan. Its culture represents a melding of beliefs and traditions from the many peoples who passed through the region. Just as the people of Pakistan have many different ethnicities and speak many different languages, they also have different traditional cultures.

In Pakistan, traditional ways are beginning to give way to a more modern culture, especially in large cities. Many urban young people are excited about these changes. But others are wary. Frequently, government officials have discouraged the free expression of artists because they do not welcome criticism of political regimes. Radical religious conservatives are also highly suspicious of many elements of popular culture in Pakistan, which they believe are a threat to the principles of Islam.

Opposite: **Classical dance in Pakistan sometimes use stylized hand gestures that help tell a story.**

The National Art Gallery

In 2007, the National Art Gallery in the Pakistani capital of Islamabad opened its doors. The four-story museum, constructed from red and yellow bricks, has more than six hundred works created by contemporary Pakistani artists. Nearly two-thirds of the artists represented are women, because the vast majority of art students in Pakistan are female.

Although the Pakistani government funds the gallery, the art it features is edgy and sometimes controversial. The museum even has an entire gallery dedicated to paintings of nudes, which is highly unusual in a Muslim country. Some of the artwork includes political statements about subjects such as Pakistan's long history of military rule and the killing of Iraqi civilians by U.S. soldiers. One of the most arresting pieces appears just outside the gallery entrance. The sculp-

ture "Seven Feelings Against Destruction" (above) by Rabia Zuberi consists of seven figures posed in a plea for peace. Another striking sculpture is Jamil Baloch's black fiberglass women. Each of the six figures in the artwork is 10 feet (3 m) tall and dressed head to toe in a burka, the controversial clothing favored by Muslim conservatives.

Films and Television

Pakistan's film industry provides a good example of how government censors and religious radicals have affected the artistic scene. In the 1960s and 1970s, the country had a bustling film industry based in Lahore. It was nicknamed Lollywood, a play on Bollywood, as India's film industry in Mumbai is often called.

Lollywood was dealt a major blow in recent years, as most of Pakistan's movie theaters closed. They could not compete with pirated DVDs and cable television. The film industry also fell into disarray because, under General Zia-ul-Haq, government policies actively discouraged moviemaking in an effort to please radical religious groups. Now, only a few dozen films are produced in Pakistan each year. Some people are trying to change this. Pakistani director Syed Noor is hoping to revive Lollywood by opening the Paragon Academy of Performing Arts (PAPA) to instruct young Pakistanis in filmmaking and acting.

Television in Pakistan has long been dominated by the Pakistan Television Corporation Network (PTV), which is owned by the government. Shows on the PTV often promote a pro-government message. But the amount and type of television programs Pakistanis can see have changed greatly with the arrival of cable television. Pakistanis can now watch a variety of private commercial networks as well as shows pro-

Men stop in at an electronics store to watch a cricket match.

duced in other countries. Popular television programs include news shows, sports programming, and soap operas.

Urban dwellers are more likely than villagers to own televisions. Pakistanis in rural villages often gather in restaurants and tea shops to watch their favorite shows. The shows are helping make all Pakistanis more comfortable with modern ways, because they combine traditional and contemporary Pakistani elements.

One show, *Coke Studio*, illustrates this. Since its premiere in 2008, it has been one of Pakistan's most-watched television programs. The musical revue showcases a wide range of acts, including performers of both traditional music and contemporary songs. By promoting both well-known and up-and-coming musical artists, *Coke Studio* has helped introduce to a national audience many young performers playing new styles of music.

Multan Blue Pottery

For many centuries, Pakistani artisans have crafted beautiful metalwork, rugs, and furniture. But perhaps the best-known traditional art of Pakistan is Multan blue pottery and tiles. The ancient city of Multan has been known for its beautiful painted ceramics since medieval times. Although they incorporate paints of various hues, the bright blue paint found on these treasures is their most distinctive feature. Multan tiles decorate many historic shrines and mosques. The blue pottery is also on display in the homes of the Pakistani president, prime minister, and other dignitaries. The public can see the works of contemporary blue pottery artists at the Institute of Blue Pottery Development in Multan.

Pakistani Pop Star

When she was just fifteen, Nazia Hassan was hailed as a singing sensation. She went on to become one of the most successful artists in the history of Asian pop music. Born in Karachi in 1965, Hassan sang on several Pakistani television shows when she was a girl. During her teens, she moved to London, England, to study. There, at a party, she met Indian film director Feroz Khan, who was impressed by her expressive voice. He asked her to sing "Aap Jaisa Koi" ("If Someone Like You Comes into My Life") in his movie *Qurbani* (1980). The film became a massive hit in India and beyond, and overnight Hassan was famous throughout Asia.

Hassan's next project, the 1981 album *Disco Deewane* ("disco crazy" in Urdu), was even more successful. Although it was a hit internationally, the album was especially exciting to her young fans in Pakistan. At that time, President Zia-ul-Haq was pushing rigid religious beliefs on Pakistani society. Government officials objected to the music video of the song "Disco Deewane" because a male and a female were dancing together, even though the male was Hassan's brother Zohaib. Despite government objections, young Pakistanis embraced the song, thrilled by Hassan's appealing vocals and the music's modern blend of Eastern and Western rhythms.

Hassan continued to make albums, including *Young Tarang* (1984), which sold more than forty million copies in Asia. She and Zohaib also hosted *Music 89*, a musical television show that aired on PTV, Pakistan's state-run television channel. It launched the careers of many other Pakistani pop artists. Hassan gave to charity much of the money she made working in the entertainment industry. After receiving a law degree from the University of London, Hassan also took a job working for the United Nations in New York.

On August 13, 2000, Hassan died of cancer in London at age thirty-five. Two years after her death, she received the Pride of Performance Award, which is the highest award the government of Pakistan can give a civilian. Her family honors her memory through the Nazia Hassan Foundation. This organization provides aid to the poor and to children in need.

Poetry and Music

Traditionally, the art form most associated with Pakistan is poetry. Poetry has a long history in the country. For example, a favorite poetic form called the *ghazal* originated in ancient times. Ghazals are romantic poems in which poets express their sadness about being separated from their beloved.

Pakistani poets of the past and present write in many languages, including Urdu, Punjabi, Sindhi, Balochi, Pashto, and

Nusrat Fateh Ali Khan introduced qawwali, spiritual songs, to people around the world. He was renowned for his energetic performances that lasted hours.

English. People throughout Pakistan are avid poetry readers. Poetry lovers also enjoy attending *mushairas*. At these events, poets perform their works for enthusiastic audiences.

In Pakistan, poetry is often sung to music. One notable example is the *qawwali*, which are spiritual songs of love and longing. One of the best-known qawwali singers was Nusrat Fateh Ali Khan. Called the King of Kings of Qawwali, his records helped build an international audience for qawwali music in the late twentieth century. Qawwali singers are often accompanied by music played on the harmonium, a keyboard instrument, and the *dhol*, a traditional two-sided drum.

In recent decades, many Pakistani performers have combined traditional song styles with contemporary musical genres. Rock and hip-hop are especially popular. Many of Pakistan's favorite pop stars gained fame by singing songs for films before the decline of the movie industry in the 1980s.

Playing Sports

For many Pakistanis, playing sports is the best possible way to relax and have fun. In school gyms and in open fields, teams get together to play field hockey and football, the game known in the United States as soccer. Badminton and table tennis (also called Ping-Pong) are popular as well.

In rural villages, Pakistanis still enjoy the traditional games of their ancestors. In the Punjab province, *kabaddi* is a favorite. In this game, two teams take turns sending a raider into the other team. During a play, the raider tries to touch as many of the opponents as possible, all the time holding his or her breath. Village children also enjoy *guli danda*, a game in which players use a large stick (called a *danda*) to hit a smaller stick (called a *guli*) into the air.

Wealthier Pakistanis in large cities often join clubs with sporting facilities. There, members can use courts for racket sports, swim in a private pool, or ride horses. Cities also have golf courses enjoyed by locals and tourists.

Pakistani athletes have had great success in the racket game called squash. Pakistanis dominated the sport from 1950 to 1997. Jahangir Khan, who was born in Karachi in 1963, is often considered the greatest squash player in history. He did not lose a single game between 1981 and 1986, winning 555 in a row.

Polo is a sport played by some elite Pakistanis. In this game, teams of horse-riding players use a mallet to move a ball and hit it into a goal. Numerous polo tournaments are played in northern areas of the country, including one held each August to celebrate Pakistan Independence Day.

Pakistani players (in green) race for the ball against Indian players in a polo match. The game of polo began in central Asia.

Cricket Hero

Imran Khan became a legend by leading Pakistan's national cricket team to victory in the 1992 World Cup tournament. Khan was born in Lahore in 1952. When he was nineteen, he began his career as a cricket player. Khan was on Pakistan's team for more than two decades, often serving as its captain. His enormous skill on the field and his good looks made him a favorite with fans. He retired from the sport at age thirty-nine, just after Pakistan's World Cup win secured his place as an international cricket superstar.

Khan has since used his fame to collect funds for charitable causes. He helped found the Shaukat Khanum Memorial Cancer Hospital and Research Centre in Lahore and Namal College in Mianwali. Khan has also established a new career in politics. In 1996, he founded his own political party, Pakistan Tehreek-e-Insaf (Pakistan Movement for Justice). Between 2002 and 2007, Khan represented Mianwali in the National Assembly.

In the past, political insiders have been quick to discount Khan's party, largely because Khan is its only member to have been elected to political office. So, many people were surprised in October 2011 when Khan led an antigovernment rally in Lahore that was attended by more than one hundred thousand people. Khan is highly critical of the government of President Asif Ali Zardari and of Pakistan's two leading political parties, the Pakistan Peoples Party and the Pakistan Muslim League. Demanding a more democratic government and an end to political corruption, Khan is attracting many supporters, especially among young people eager to see drastic reforms in Pakistan's political system.

The most popular sport in Pakistan is cricket. The British introduced cricket to South Asia in the eighteenth century. The game is something like baseball and is played by two teams on a large grass field. Each team has eleven players. The players use bats and balls to try to score runs. A game of cricket sometimes lasts for several days.

Throughout Pakistan, amateurs play games of cricket for big crowds. Fans everywhere also cheer for their national team, which plays teams from countries around the world. In 1992, Pakistan won the prestigious Cricket World Cup.

Sporting Events

Throughout Pakistan, special annual sporting events draw big audiences. One such event is the Lahore Horse and Cattle Show. Sponsored by the government of Punjab, it features displays of livestock—including many breeds of cattle and buffalo—as well as trick horseback riding, dog racing, and dances performed by horses and camels.

Recently, the Cholistan Desert Jeep Rally, first held in 2005, has helped popularize motor sports in Pakistan. This event brings locals and tourists to Pakistan's southern desert lands to watch a series of jeep races.

Roughly every two years, some of the world's premiere cyclists gather in Karachi to participate in the Tour de Pakistan, a bike race modeled on the famous Tour de France. The course, which stretches for more than 1,000 miles (1,600 km), makes it the longest of any bike race held in Asia.

In early March, the Pakistani city of Lahore celebrates the

coming of spring with the Basant Festival. A high point of the festivities is the kite flying contests. People gather in open fields and on rooftops to fly kites of all shapes and sizes. During the competitions, two kite fliers go head-to-head. The string of each kite is coated with ground glass. To win the battle, a flier tries to aim his or her kite so that the glass-coated string cuts the competitor's kite string. When one kite slashes the string of another, the crowd cheers the victor as children race to catch the falling kite.

People fly all kinds of kites at the Basant Festival. This kite is 30 x 50 feet (9 x 15 m).

The Pakistani Way

PAKISTAN IS EXPERIENCING A TIME OF RAPID CHANGE. As more of its population moves to urban areas, the lives of many Pakistanis are going through a transformation. There is not just one Pakistani way of life. Certainly, the daily life of a professional living in the busy city of Lahore has little in common with a farmer working the land in a small remote village on the Balochistan Plateau. Even so, no matter where they live, most Pakistanis still have some things in common—from the clothes they wear to the foods they enjoy to their strong devotion to their families.

Opposite: **A man sips tea at a market in Peshawar.**

Living Together

In cities, Pakistanis tend to live in modest apartments or town houses. In rural areas, they generally live in small flat-topped houses made from mud or bricks. Remote villages usually do not have access to electricity or modern plumbing. Instead, people rely on well water for cooking and washing.

Pakistanis pride themselves on their hospitality. When guests come to their homes, they do everything they can to make the visitors feel comfortable and welcome. Wealthier families often reserve a room in their house just for entertaining guests.

Many Pakistani households include relatives from several generations. Often grandparents, parents, and children share the same house. From a young age, children are taught to respect their older relatives. At any gathering, elders are greeted first and served food and drink before anyone else.

On average, Pakistani men live to age sixty-five, and Pakistani women live to age sixty-eight.

Women working at a post office in Karachi. Only about 22 percent of Pakistani women work outside the home.

Men also have a privileged role within the family. Generally, fathers make important decisions on behalf of their wives and children. They often decide what children study in school and which profession they will enter when they grow up. Men are expected to support their extended families financially, but women usually do the day-to-day work of running the household and caring for the children.

In the past, nearly all Pakistani women worked at home, sometimes also helping with a family business or farm. Increasingly, though, women are taking on full-time jobs. Many work in fields traditionally dominated by women, such as teaching and nursing. Increasingly, others have jobs in offices, banks, hotels, and industry.

A father and son in Kashmir. The average family in Pakistan has three children.

Raising Children

In Pakistan, when a child is born, the father celebrates by giving sweets in colorful boxes to friends and relatives. The mother might put a *ta'weez* around the baby's neck. This is a charm thought to protect children from illness and harm.

From a very early age, girls are expected to help their mothers with running the household. Boys are often indulged with more playtime. They are also more likely to go to school. Parents want boys to get an education, because when they grow up, the boys will be expected to help support the parents in their old age. Even if a grown son lives far away, he feels obligated to send money home.

The constitution of Pakistan states that children have a right to a primary school education (grades one through five). But only two-thirds of young Pakistanis graduate from primary school. Students who continue their education spend three years in middle school and four years in high school. For higher education, they may attend one of the many colleges and universities in the country.

The education average Pakistanis receive often depends on their gender and where they live. Boys are more likely to be sent to school than girls are. About 69 percent of men can read and write, while only 45 percent of women can. People in cities tend to be better educated than those in rural areas, because villagers often need their children to work to help support their families. About 74 percent of city dwellers are literate, but just less than half of rural residents are.

The University of the Punjab in Lahore was established in 1882. It is one of the oldest universities in Pakistan.

Getting Married

When children grow up, they usually remain in their parents' home until they get married. Parents are often responsible for finding spouses for their adult children. In rural areas, a bride and groom might not even meet each other before the wedding.

Oonch Neech

Pakistani children play a game called Oonch Neech, which roughly means "up and down." The game begins with one player being selected as "it." This player chases the other children, trying to tag them. A player who is tagged becomes the new "it." Players are safe from being tagged if they manage to climb on anything—from a rock to a tree to a jungle gym—that allows them to keep their feet off the ground.

Such arranged marriages are normal for conservative families, but they are also common among people who live a less traditional way of life. In Pakistan, marriage is considered not just a bond between two people, but a bond between two families.

The expense of a traditional wedding generally falls on the bride's family. Wedding ceremonies are elaborate. Festivities can continue for several days, during which many guests must be fed and entertained.

A bride and groom walk to their wedding ceremony surrounded by relatives.

Henna Party

Traditionally, the day before a Pakistani wedding, the bride and her female friends get together for the Rasm-e-Hina, or henna party. Henna is a reddish-brown dye made from leaves of the mignonette tree. As the bride sits on a stool in a beautiful, colorful dress, her friends gather around her, carrying a decorated tray with the henna paste. They apply the henna on her hands and feet in floral designs. Sometimes, her fiancé's name is incorporated into the designs. The guests also sing and dance well into the night to celebrate their friend's upcoming wedding and wish her a joyful marriage.

The bride's relatives must also come up with the dowry. A dowry is a payment of money or goods that a bride gives to the groom when they get married. In contemporary Pakistan, a dowry might include jewelry, a television set, a car, or even a house.

Often, a family will begin saving for a girl's dowry as soon as she is born. Poor Pakistani parents sometimes take out loans for a dowry. Although the debt is a heavy burden, in the long run it costs less than supporting an unmarried daughter for the rest of her life.

Public Holidays

February 5	Kashmir Day
March 23	Pakistan Day
May 1	Labor Day
August 14	Independence Day
November 9	Birthday of Muhammad Iqbal
December 25	Birthday of Mohammed Ali Jinnah

Many Pakistani teenagers wear a shalwar kameez as their school uniform.

Clothing and Dress

The standard clothing for many Pakistanis, both men and women, is the *shalwar kameez*. A kameez is a long tunic, usually made out of cotton. It is worn over the shalwar, a pair of light, baggy pants. These garments are practical given Pakistan's climate, because they are comfortable during both cool winters and hot summers.

Women sometimes wear a *dupatta*. This long scarf is commonly draped over the chest and down the back. Sometimes a woman places it over her head as a show of respect, such as in the presence of elders. Often, women wear their hair tied back into a long braid. In cities, though, many women favor shorter, more modern hairstyles.

Some city dwellers have given up traditional dress altogether. They wear fashionable suits and dresses like those seen on residents of European and American cities. In contrast, very religiously conservative Pakistani women wear burkas. These loose-fitting, head-to-toe garments cover the entire body, except for a small open slit at the eyes that allows the woman to see where she's going.

Some Pakistani women wear burkas in public. These garments cover their bodies completely.

Pakistan's cuisine, like that of neighboring India, is known for flavorful mixes of spices. Many favorite dishes and stews combine meats, such as lamb, chicken, beef, or goat, with fresh vegetables. Pakistani Muslims do not eat pork because Islam forbids it.

The staple food of Pakistan is bread. Fresh bread made from wheat flour is featured at virtually every meal. A common type of bread is called *naan*. It is a flatbread that is cooked in a clay oven. Other breads enjoyed by Pakistanis include *roti*, *chapati*, and *paratha*.

A man carries stacks of naan. In Pakistan, nuts, raisins, or sesame seeds are often added to naan.

Pakistani pulao is often flavored with spices such as cinnamon, cloves, and cardamom.

For breakfast, Pakistanis often eat *nihari*, which is an Urdu word meaning "morning." It is made of chunks of meat that are cooked overnight and mixed with spices and chilis. Lunch might be a kebab, a skewer of meat cooked over an open grill. Dishes served for dinner include *keema* (minced meat flavored with onion, garlic, and spices), *kofte* (spiced meatballs), and *pulao* (rice in broth with meat or potatoes).

Pakistanis often enjoy samosas with a meal or as a snack. These are deep-fried triangular pastries, usually filled with potatoes, onions, and peas. Pakistanis also enjoy a wide variety of sweets. A favorite is *gajar ka halwa*, a hot wintertime treat made from sugar, carrots, and cream.

The most popular beverage in Pakistan is tea. It is usually strongly brewed and mixed with milk, sugar, and sometimes spices, such as cardamom. Pakistani men often while away

Lassi

Lassi is a popular summer drink in Pakistan. Traditionally, lassi is seasoned with spices and salt. But in modern times, Pakistanis have also come to enjoy sweet lassi, often for breakfast. You can make a simple version of sweet lassi with ingredients you might already have in your house.

Ingredients

1 cup plain yogurt

¼ cup water

1 tablespoon sugar

Fresh fruit chunks (banana, strawberry, pineapple, or mango, etc.)

¼ cup crushed ice

Instructions

Put the yogurt and water into a blender. Blend for about 45 seconds. Add the sugar and fruit, and blend until well mixed. Place the crushed ice into a tall glass, and pour the blended mixture over it. Enjoy!

hours at a time, drinking tea and chatting with their friends at the country's tea stalls.

Pakistanis purchase much of their food and other necessities at outdoor shopping areas called bazaars. Some sell a wide variety of goods, while others specialize in a specific type of merchandise, such as shoes or carpets. Usually, there is no set price for goods sold at bazaars. Customers haggle, or bargain, with shopkeepers in the hope of getting a particularly good deal.

News and Technology

To get news about Pakistan and the world beyond, Pakistanis read many newspapers and magazines. Newspapers are available in more than ten languages, although most papers are

Many Pakistanis still get their news from papers, even as Internet use increases.

published in Urdu, Sindhi, and English. Pakistanis can also get the news of the day from radio shows and television programs. The government runs many radio and TV stations, and as a result much of their news has a pro-government bias. Although the constitution guarantees freedom of the press, it also allows the government to restrict what reporters say about Islam and national security issues. Often, journalists censor themselves for fear of getting in trouble with government officials. But increasingly, private stations, particularly those broadcasting from foreign countries, are providing Pakistanis with other perspectives.

Urban Pakistanis also turn to the Internet for news, although officials block some Web sites. About twenty million people in

Young Pakistanis at a computer class

Pakistan are Internet users. Cell phone users are much more common. In recent years, access to cell phones has skyrocketed. In 2000, just three hundred thousand Pakistanis had cell phones. By 2011, that number had spiked to more than one hundred million. Cell phones have been particularly welcomed in rural areas where traditional phone lines are unavailable.

As more Pakistanis are introduced to these and other technologies, the pace of change is becoming more rapid than ever. Pakistanis have long been a divided people, deeply separated by ethnicity, culture, and language. Now there are additional tensions between those who have access to new technologies and those who do not. Bridging this gulf is just one of the many challenges Pakistan faces as it struggles to build a more prosperous and peaceful future for its people.

Ninety percent of Pakistanis live in areas that have cell phone coverage.

Timeline

Pakistani History		World History	
The Harappan culture reaches its height in the Indus River valley.	ca. 2600-1900 BCE	ca. 2500 BCE	Egyptians build the pyramids and the Sphinx in Giza.
		ca. 563 BCE	The Buddha is born in India.
Pakistan becomes part of the Mauryan Empire.	300 BCE	313 CE	The Roman emperor Constantine legalizes Christianity.
Arab invaders introduce Islam to what is now southern Pakistan.	711 CE	610	The Prophet Muhammad begins preaching a new religion called Islam.
		1054	The Eastern (Orthodox) and Western (Roman Catholic) Churches break apart.
		1095	The Crusades begin.
		1215	King John seals the Magna Carta.
		1300s	The Renaissance begins in Italy.
		1347	The plague sweeps through Europe.
		1453	Ottoman Turks capture Constantinople, conquering the Byzantine Empire.
		1492	Columbus arrives in North America.
The Mughal Empire emerges on the Indian subcontinent.	1500s	1500s	Reformers break away from the Catholic Church, and Protestantism is born.
		1776	The U.S. Declaration of Independence is signed.
		1789	The French Revolution begins.
The British establish rule over India (including present-day Pakistan).	1858	1865	The American Civil War ends.
		1879	The first practical lightbulb is invented.
		1914	World War I begins.
		1917	The Bolshevik Revolution brings communism to Russia.

Pakistani History

Poet and politician Muhammad Iqbal proposes a Muslim state within an independent India.	1930
The All-India Muslim League supports the creation of Pakistan.	1940
India is partitioned to create East and West Pakistan.	1947
Liaquat Ali Khan, Pakistan's first prime minister, is assassinated.	1951
General Muhammad Ayub Khan stages a coup and becomes Pakistan's first military ruler.	1958
Pakistan and India go to war over disputed lands in Kashmir.	1965
Civil war breaks out when East Pakistan secedes; East Pakistan becomes the independent nation of Bangladesh.	1971
General Zia-ul-Haq takes control of the government and promotes a strict form of Islam.	1977
The United States offers Pakistan aid to help fight Soviet forces in Afghanistan.	1980
Benazir Bhutto becomes the first female prime minister of Pakistan.	1988
Pakistan conducts its first nuclear tests.	1998
General Pervez Musharraf reestablishes military rule.	1999
An earthquake in Pakistan-administered Kashmir kills tens of thousands of people.	2005
Benazir Bhutto is assassinated.	2007
President Musharraf resigns under pressure.	2008
American soldiers kill Osama bin Laden, the mastermind behind the September 11 attacks, in Abbottabad.	2011

World History

1929	A worldwide economic depression begins.
1939	World War II begins.
1945	World War II ends.
1957	The Vietnam War begins.
1969	Humans land on the Moon.
1975	The Vietnam War ends.
1989	The Berlin Wall is torn down as communism crumbles in Eastern Europe.
1991	The Soviet Union breaks into separate states.
2001	Terrorists attack the World Trade Center in New York City and the Pentagon near Washington, D.C.
2004	A tsunami in the Indian Ocean destroys coastlines in Africa, India, and Southeast Asia.
2008	The United States elects its first African American president.

Fast Facts

Official name: Islamic Republic of Pakistan

Capital: Islamabad

Official language: Urdu

Karachi

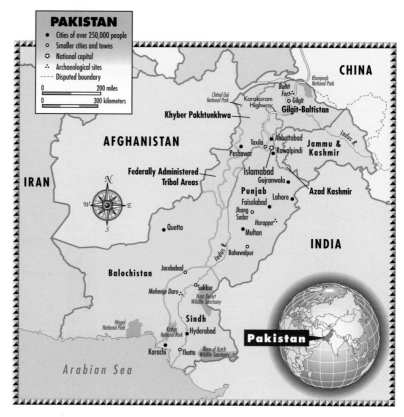

Pakistani Flag

Official religion:	Islam
Year of founding:	1947
National anthem:	"Qaumi Tarana" ("National Anthem")
Government:	Federal republic
Chief of state:	President
Head of government:	Prime minister
Area:	307,374 square miles (796,095 sq km)
Latitude and longitude of geographic center:	30° N, 70° E
Bordering countries:	Iran to the west; Afghanistan to the north and west; China to the north; and India to the east
Highest elevation:	K2, 28,251 feet (8,611 m) above sea level
Lowest elevation:	Indian Ocean, sea level
Highest average temperature:	106°F (41°C) in June
Lowest average temperature:	41°F (5°C) in January
National population (2011 est.):	190,291,129

Himalayas

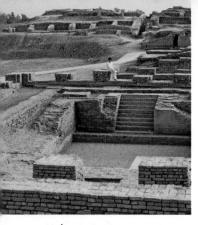

Mohenjo Daro

Population of largest cities (2010 est.):

Karachi	13,205,339
Lahore	7,129,609
Faisalabad	2,990,675
Rawalpindi	1,409,768
Multan	1,197,384

Landmarks:
- ▶ *Faisal Mosque,* Islamabad
- ▶ *Lahore Fort,* Lahore
- ▶ *Mohenjo Daro,* Sindh province
- ▶ *Shalamar Gardens,* Lahore
- ▶ *Shish Mahal,* Lahore

Economy: About 40 percent of Pakistanis work in agriculture. Important crops grown in Pakistan include wheat, rice, sugarcane, and cotton. Pakistan's industrial exports include textiles, chemicals, processed food, fertilizer, leather goods, and sports equipment. Banking, communications, and retail sales dominate the service sector.

Currency: The rupee. In 2012, US$1.00 equaled about 90 rupees.

System of weights and measures: Metric system

Literacy rate (2005 est.): 50 percent

Currency

Schoolchildren

Benazir Bhutto

Common Urdu words and phrases:

Kya haal hae?	How are you?
T'heek hoon	I am fine
Assalam aléikum	God's peace be with you (greeting)
Wa'al éikum salam	And with you too (response to greeting)
Khodáh hafíz	God be with you (good-bye)
Shúkri'a	Thank you
Bóhat shúkri'a	Thank you very much

Prominent Pakistanis:

Benazir Bhutto (1953–2007)
Prime minister

Muhammad Iqbal (1877–1938)
Poet and politician

Mohammed Ali Jinnah (1876–1948)
Political leader

Imran Khan (1952–)
Cricket player and politician

Nusrat Fateh Ali Khan (1948–1997)
Singer

To Find Out More

Books

▶ Egendorf, Laura K., ed. *Pakistan*. Detroit, MN: Greenhaven Press, 2010.

▶ Harmon, Daniel E. Pervez Musharraf: *President of Pakistan*. New York: Rosen Publishing, 2007.

▶ Kovarik, Chiara Angela. *Interviews with Muslim Women of Pakistan*. Minneapolis, MN: Syren Book Company, 2005.

▶ Sheen, Barbara. *Foods of Pakistan*. Detroit, MN: KidHaven Press, 2011.

Music

▶ Hassan, Nazia, and Zoheb Hassan. *Young Tarang*. Hom/Crescendo, 2008.

▶ Khan, Nusrat Fateh Ali. *Mustt Mustt*. Real World Records, 1990.

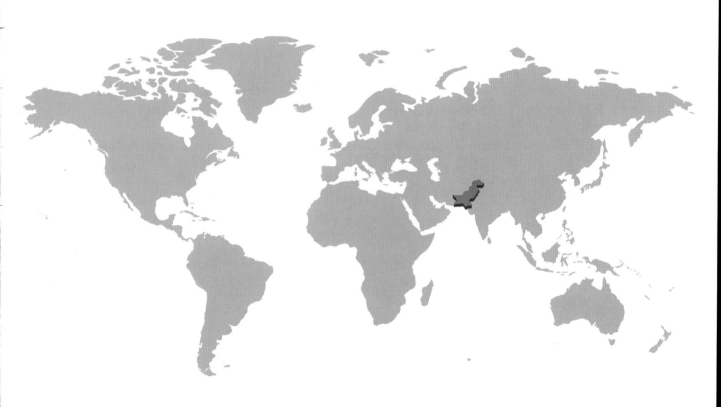

▶ Visit this Scholastic Web site for more information on Pakistan:
www.factsfornow.scholastic.com
Enter the keyword **Pakistan**

Index

Page numbers in *italics*
indicate illustrations.

Urdu language, 41, 44, 84, 86–88, 87, 88, 89, 89, 105, 126

V

villages. *See also* cities.
    Harappa, 10
    Khaplu, *26*
    sports in, 107
    television in, 104
    well water, 113

W

weights and measures, 70
West Pakistan, 44–45, 49
wheat, 21, 28, 68, 69, 70, 75, 122
wildlife. *See* animal life; marine life;
    plant life; reptilian life.
women, 50–51, *54*, *55*, 66, 66, 67,
    115, *115*, 119, *119*, 121, *121*
World War II, 43
World Wildlife Fund, 35

Y

Yahya Khan, Muhammad, 48, 49

Z

Zardari, Asif Ali, 52, 60, 66, 66, 109
Zia-ul-Haq, Muhammad, 49–50, *49*,
    51, 66, 102, 105

Meet the Author

A GRADUATE OF SWARTHMORE COLLEGE, LIZ Sonneborn is a full-time writer living in Brooklyn, New York. She has written more than ninety nonfiction books for both children and adults on a wide variety of subjects. Her works include *The American West*, *A to Z of American Indian Women*, *The Ancient Kushites*, *The Vietnamese Americans*, *Chronology of American Indian History*, *Guglielmo Marconi*, and *The Environmental Movement*.

Sonneborn is a veteran of the Enchantment of the World series. She has written four other volumes—*Canada*, *Iraq*, *United Arab Emirates*, and *Yemen*—in addition to *Pakistan*. To research all of these books, she employed a similar strategy. She started with general sources to get a basic understanding of the country and its history and culture, and then sought out resources that explored specific issues, particularly those likely to interest young people the most. She faced several challenges in writing about contemporary Pakistan. One was that the people of Pakistan today live very different lives depending on factors such as where they live, their ethnic group,

their gender, their embrace of modern ways, and more. Another challenge was the rapid pace of change in the country. Politically and culturally, Pakistan is a place in flux. To get a grasp on this changing world, the Internet was a vital research tool. Of course, the Internet offers an incredible number of up-to-the-minute newspaper and magazine articles at the touch of a keyboard. But Sonneborn also found the vast array of available visual media—from YouTube news clips to movie trailers—to be very useful in helping her get an accurate picture of contemporary Pakistan.

Sonneborn was interested in learning more about Pakistan and its history for a personal reason. "When I was in middle school and high school in the 1970s," she explains, "I had several friends who were refugees from Pakistan and Bangladesh. From them, I learned a little about their native lands, but I was excited to have the chance to really delve into the subject. I also had a Pakistani friend in college who, whenever she visited her parents, brought back a plateful of incredibly spicy homemade samosas to share with her dorm mates. Silly but true, there's nothing like delicious snacks to make you want to find out more about a foreign culture."

Photo Credits